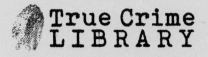

ORGANIZED CRIME

DRUG CARTELS AND SMUGGLERS
INFAMOUS TERRORISTS
MASS MURDERERS
MODERN-DAY PIRATES
ORGANIZED CRIME
SERIAL KILLERS

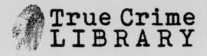

True Crime
LIBRARY

ORGANIZED
CRIME

JIM WHITING

ELDORADO INK

Eldorado Ink
PO Box 100097
Pittsburgh, PA 15233
www.eldoradoink.com

Produced by OTTN Publishing, Stockton, New Jersey

CPSIA compliance information: Batch#CS2013-5. For further information, contact Eldorado Ink at info@eldoradoink.com.

First printing

1 3 5 7 9 8 6 4 2

Library of Congress Cataloging-in-Publication Data
available from the Library of Congress

ISBN-13: 978-1-61900-040-7 (hc)
ISBN-13: 978-1-61900-041-4 (trade)
ISBN-13: 978-1-61900-042-1 (ebook)

*For information about custom editions, special sales, or premiums,
please contact our special sales department at info@eldoradoink.com.*

TABLE OF CONTENTS

Liborio "Barney" Belloma
Acting Boss

ny "Rom" Romanello
Acting Capo

John "Buster" Ardito
Capo

A police diagram shows members of the Genovese organized crime family in New York after their 2006 indictment on charges of murder, money laundering and drug distribution. Over the past 75 years, organized crime in the United States was dominated by Italian-American crime families, often referred to collectively as "the mob," "mafia," or "la cosa nostra." Since the 1990s new criminal organizations have emerged to challenge the mob for control of many criminal activities.

ORGANIZED CRIME
AN INTRODUCTION

Organized crime and the people associated with it have long been a subject of public fascination. This fascination has been fueled by books, television, and the movies. Yet even though it is so highly publicized, organized crime can be difficult to define. Violent urban street gangs such as the Crips or the Latin Kings are not necessarily involved in organized crime. Nor are infamous outlaws like Jesse James, bank robbers like John Dillinger, or drug traffickers like Pablo Escobar.

The term *organized crime* is used to refer to complex network of criminals who work together in a systematic way to make money through criminal activity. Often, the criminal organization—sometimes called a "crime family" or a "mob"—controls illegal activity that is ongoing, such as underground gambling or prostitution rings, within a large region of the country. Sometimes the group controls this illegal activity on a national scale.

In a way, these criminal organizations are like businesses—their primary goal is to make money. Also, like a modern corporation, crime families have a strict hierarchy—there is a boss at the top, who gives orders to underbosses, who in turn control larger groups of lower-level gang members that carry out the boss's orders. The families are disciplined, and members are not permitted to engage in criminal activities without first getting the boss's permission.

Crime families are different from legitimate businesses in another important way. They are not afraid to use violence against those who might try to prevent them from making their illegal profits. They also bribe corrupt public officials so that they will not interfere with their moneymaking schemes.

Officials who refuse to take bribes may be threatened or blackmailed to leave the crime family alone.

The term *racketeering* is used to describe the illegal activities of crime families. A *racket* is an illegal business or scheme. In the early 20th century, one common scheme was the "protection racket." This is a form of extortion in which a mobster requires local business owners to pay him money on a regular basis. In exchange, the mobster promises to protect the business from harm. If a business owner refuses, the mobster and his associates will come back and cause damage to the business, smashing shop windows or destroying merchandise. In this way, the mobster intimidates merchants into paying the "protection" fees. These schemes often target small businesses, such as neighborhood grocery stores or restaurants.

However, some schemes involving large corporations threatened with labor unrest have resulted in million-dollar payoffs to the mob.

Some of the other rackets that crime families have been involved with include smuggling and distributing illegal alcohol and drugs; managing underground gambling games; making high-interest loans (a practice known as "loan sharking"); running prostitution rings; and control of worker unions (known as "labor racketeering.")

DRUG AND ALCOHOL DISTRIBUTION

Most of the modern crime families were formed during a time when it was illegal to produce, sell, or consume alcohol in the United States. This period, known as Prohibition, began in January 1920. The Prohibition laws were intended to reduce crime and improve American

Federal prohibition agents destroy the bar in a speakeasy during the 1920s. During the Prohibition era (1920-1933), bootlegging was so profitable that many criminal groups tried to become involved. The resulting rivalries between gangs led to violence as gangs defended their territories and their illegal shipments of alcohol. In major cities like Chicago, New York, and Detroit, there were hundreds of gang-related murders each year.

morals. Instead, they had the opposite effect, creating a secret culture of crime.

Despite the laws, many Americans—especially those who lived in the cities—still thirsted for beer, wine, and whiskey, and they were willing to purchase it illegally. Smuggling alcohol into the country from Canada (where brewing and distilling were still legal) and selling it in underground nightclubs known as "speakeasies," became an extremely lucrative criminal business.

The first smuggling, or "bootlegging" efforts were done on a small scale. However, it was soon apparent that huge amounts of money could be made by those who were able to supply alcohol. In many American cities street gangs became more organized, creating networks to smuggle the illegal alcohol into their area and distribute it to their customers.

Prohibition was a federal law, but in the 1920s there was no government agency with the manpower to enforce the law. Local police were supposed to stop the distribution of illegal alcohol, but bootlegging brought in so much money that gang leaders were able to use some to bribe policemen, judges, and other public officials to look the other way.

During the 1920s, the primary risk for bootleggers came from rival gangs, which would try to hijack their illegal

A Prohibition agent destroys kegs of confiscated beer, 1924.

shipments of alcohol. It was not uncommon for the unfortunate men driving the trucks to be murdered. The gangs fought for control of territories where they could sell their alcohol.

Eventually, the crime and murders associated with bootlegging forced the federal government to take action against the gangs. Federal prosecutors targeted gang leaders and tried to disrupt their illegal activities. In 1933, the Prohibition laws were repealed. Legalizing alcohol removed a significant

The iconic Thompson submachine gun—known colloquially as the "Tommy gun"—was the favored weapon of Prohibition-era gunmen.

source of illicit revenue for the mobs. But by this time many of the mobs were strong enough to simply expand into other illegal businesses.

One venture that some crime families became involved in was distributing illegal drugs such as heroin, cocaine, and marijuana. The market for drugs was relatively small in the 1930s, but gradually increased as organized crime groups made it more readily available. Today, crime families often work with international drug cartels to control the distribution of illegal drugs in their territories.

GAMBLING AND LOAN SHARKING

Illegal gambling has long been a source of revenue for organized crime families. In urban America during the late 19th century, immigrants played the "numbers racket." This was a type of lottery, in which people would bet on a random three-digit number. A bookie would take bets, usually from a public location such as a parking lot or a storefront. Runners—typically a young person who was just getting their start in a gang—would carry the money from the betting location to a central headquarters.

"Betting the numbers" was popular among poor immigrants because bets could be as low as a penny and a winning bet would usually pay off at odds of about 600 to 1. (This means that a person who bet $1 would be paid $600.)

Although that payoff seems generous, the chances that a person will actually choose the right three-digit number are 1,000 to 1. In other words, if a bookie takes $1,000 in bets and has to pay one winner $600, he ends up with a $400 profit.

To avoid accusations that the numbers games are not rigged in favor of the bookie, or "fixed," the number is usually a publicly published one chosen in advance. For example, during the 1930s many New York bookies used the last three digits of the total amount of money that had been wagered on a particular race at a local horse racing track, because that number was published in the daily newspaper the next day.

Although numbers games are illegal, during the 1960s and 1970s some state government began to operate their own legal lotteries. Today, 44 states operate lotteries, which pay winners at varying odds and use the funds from sales of lottery tickets to supplement taxes and pay for public programs. Despite this, some people still prefer to bet in illegal mob-run games. One reason is that they do not have to pay taxes on their winnings.

Another is that bookies are sometimes willing to extend credit to regular customers.

Another related mob practice is loan sharking, or loaning money at high interest rates to people who cannot borrow from a bank for some reason. If a person has bet on credit with a bookie and can't pay, he may have to borrow from a loan shark to avoid being physically beaten. Usually, bank or credit card loans charge an interest rate of between 3 percent and 18 percent a year on the balance owed. Loan sharks often lend at much higher rates—10 percent to 20 percent a week! In some cases they begin with a rate that seems reasonable, then quickly raise it to exorbitant levels. Failure to repay the loan can result in injury or death to the recipients of the loan and/or their families.

The Federal Bureau of Investigation (FBI) defines organized crime as "any group having some manner of a formalized structure and whose primary objective is to obtain money through illegal activities. Such groups maintain their position through the use of actual or threatened violence, corrupt public officials, graft, or extortion, and generally have a significant impact on the people in their locales, region, or the country as a whole."

During the 1940s, the state of Nevada passed laws that made gambling legal. Soon, the mob moved into places like Las Vegas and Reno and created a flourishing gambling industry. Crime families invested heavily in casinos, and were able to skim millions in profits that could be used to purchase other legitimate businesses, as well as pay for illegal activities. Eventually, the government began to regulate casinos more tightly, so that known mobsters could not be involved.

PROSTITUTION AND HUMAN TRAFFICKING

Prostitution, the exchange of money for sex, has been called the "world's oldest profession." Prostitution is illegal in most U.S. states, and organized crime has always taken advantage of the demand for this. Crime families run ille-

Mob leaders made enormous profits from running casinos because the odds of virtually every casino game are tilted slightly in the house's favor. For example, in roulette if the ball drops into one of two green slots (numbered 0 and 00), the house wins all the money that has been bet on red/black or on any other number. That provides about a five percent edge to the casino, which means that over time the house is assured of winning at least $5 for every $100 wagered. Other casino games, such as slot machines, have an even higher edge for the house of 15 to 25 percent. By the mid-1950s, when the mob controlled most of the casinos in Las Vegas, Americans were gambling more than $200 million a year there, meaning tens of millions in profit for the gangsters.

(Right) Federal agents compiled this list of brothels in Tacoma, Washington, in 1932. Several of the establishments are noted to be selling liquor illegally.

(Bottom) Human trafficking involves the use of force, fraud, or coercion to enslave a person. The U.S. Department of State estimates between 600,000 and 800,000 people are trafficked across international borders each year. About 65 percent are forced into prostitution.

The following resorts are all operating openly, as houses of prostitution, or liquor dispensing places. They are all within eleven blocks of the city hall, and openly boast of the fact that they pay money for protection. The amount of protection money variesfrom $150 to $350, and is supposed to be paid before the 8th of each month. Up until April of this year, the collection was made by Mike Vendetti, who about two years ago served a six months sentence for liquor violation. Since April the collections have been made by Primo Rosellini, who served a penitentiary sentence of one year for narcotic violation. These collections are all made in the name of Vito Cuttone, who is supposed to be the chief fixer:

1. Holly Hotel, 811 Pacific Avenue, Owner, Claude Judge--2 prostitutes, and liquor sold.

2. Camp Hotel, 1205½ Pacific Avenue, Owner, Ida Kline (jewess)--4 to 6 prostitutes.

3. McBeth Hotel, 1215½ Pacific Avenue, formerly known as the St. Charles Hotel, originally owned by Vito Cuttone-sold to Lil Hart (negress), who served a California penitentiary sentence about four years ago. Lil Hart sold this place to Blanche Davis (jewess) about six months ago, who now has another jewess operating the place with two prostitutes and sells liquor.

4. Doris Hotel, 1217½ Pacific Avenue, owned by Sam Levine (jew), operated by his wife with from 4 to 6 prostitutes.

5. Franklin Hotel, 1317½ Pacific Avenue. Operated by Frank Mayhew--3 prostitutes and liquor sold.

6. Fern Hotel, 1319½ Pacific Avenue, owned by Blanche Davis (jewess) operated by two prostitutes known as Bee Guinan, and Sunny Boyd. Liquor sold.

cific Avenue, formerly owned by Jay Chavis (negro) sold whose name is unknown--2 and 3 prostitutes. Liquor sold.

Pacific Avenue, owned by Nick Ranich, and operated by titutes. Liquor sold.

09 Commerce Street, owned by Jack Consella, and operated utes, and liquor sold.

ny owned by Blanche Davis--3 prostitutes, and liquor sold.

h 13th, operated by large blonde woman, name unknown--2 r sold.

lor, 1302 Broadway, owner unknown. Open bar where liquor

gal brothels, where people come to have sex with prostitutes, as well as escort services that send prostitutes to the clients. In the United States, illegal prostitution is a billion-dollar business, according to the FBI, and is the mob's third-largest source of revenue.

Today many prostitutes come to America from Eastern Europe, Southeast Asia, and South America. They are lured by promises of honest work, or even marriage, in another country. Often they are still teenagers.

When they arrive, they find that the promises are bogus, and they are forced to work as prostitutes. Often, because these young women entered the country illegally, they are afraid of approaching authorities. This sort of illegal enslaving of vulnerable people is known as human trafficking.

Not all of the people who are brought illegally to the United States become prostitutes. Some are forced to take grueling jobs as migrant workers, or to work as domestic servants or in restaurants or factories. They are paid little or nothing for their work.

LABOR RACKETEERING

Labor unions are organizations of workers in a particular trade or industry. Leaders of the labor union bargain with an employer to make sure that workers are paid fairly and to ensure safe working conditions. Unions also protect workers from being fired without a good reason, or from being replaced by unskilled workers that the employer can pay less. In exchange for these benefits, workers pay dues to the union. This money is used to pay union leaders, as well as to provide health benefits and retirement pensions to union members.

These benefit funds can contain very large sums of money, making them of interest to criminal organizations. For example, the International Brotherhood of Teamsters is a union that represents 1.4 million workers in the trucking and transportation industries. It has a pension fund valued at more than $9 billion. When organized crime figures gain control of a union like the Teamsters, they can decide where that pension fund invests it money—often diverting it into legitimate businesses owned by the mob, such as construction companies, garbage disposal firms, and other industries.

The term *labor racketeering* is used to refer to the control and manipulation of a labor union. In addition to controlling union funds, crime families may use the union's ability to go on strike as a way to extort payoffs from large businesses that would be affected. The business owners will pay the mob to ensure good relations with its labor union—in effect, this is a pro-

(Left) Mobsters have been involved with labor unions since the early 20th century. They used the threat of strikes or labor unrest to extort payments from business owners. Here, police clash with striking members of the Teamsters Union in Minneapolis, 1934.

(Above) Teamsters president Jimmy Hoffa was convicted in 1964 of bribery and fraudulent use of the union's pension fund. Hoffa had close ties to organized crime. After his release from prison in 1971, Hoffa mysteriously disappeared; most people believe he was murdered by the mob.

tection racket on a large scale. These payments, of course, increase the company's expenses, and are passed on to consumers. In effect, Americans unknowingly pay mobsters what amounts to a surcharge on a wide range of goods and services.

MONEY LAUNDERING

All rackets have one thing in common: they generate large amounts of money. To prevent the government from catching on to the scope of their illegal activities, mobsters need to make it seem that their money has been earned in a legitimate business. The way in which this is done is called *money laundering*. (The term appears to have originated in the 1920s, when the infamous Chicago gangster Al Capone bought two laundry businesses. He used them as financial fronts for his illegal activities.)

It is common for crime families to invest some of their illegal profits into legitimate businesses like construction firms, restaurants and nighclubs, hotels, bakeries, waste disposal firms, shopping mall developers, and other industries. Mob bosses use these businesses to provide jobs for their soldiers, and as a cover-up for their illegal revenue.

Illegal money can also be laundered by transferring it between "shell corporations." These are companies that exist only on paper, and are chartered in foreign places with little government over-

Mob bosses can use legitimate businesses like construction companies to hide the profits from their illegal operations.

sight, such as Liberia or the Cayman Islands. The money is repeatedly transferred from one shell corporation to another as a way to disguise its crime-related origins.

ORGANIZED CRIME TODAY

Many of the chapters in this book provide background information about the beginnings of organized crime in the United States. By the early years of the 20th century, street gangs had formed in New York and other urban areas. Often, these gangs were made up of the poorest recent immigrants to the United States, and organized along ethnic lines: Irish, Jewish, Italian, Hungarian, Greek, and Slovak, to name a few. The gangs established territories, and defended them when other gangs tried to encroach on their turf.

By the early 1930s, the Italian-American mobs had become the dominant criminal organizations in most American cities. There were five Italian crime families in New York, one powerful family in Chicago, and crime families that controlled other major cities like Philadelphia, Boston, Detroit, and Los Angeles. Leaders of these crime families developed an agreement to work together and respect each family's turf, so that all the families could focus on making money through the rackets that they controlled. The agreement created a board called the Commission, which regulated disputes among the families and ensured that agreements were kept. This created a stable situation in which the mobsters could grow wealthy, and the next few decades would be a "golden age" for organized crime in America. The head of one of the New York families, Joe Bonanno, would later reflect:

> For nearly a thirty-year period after the Castellammarese War [a bloody gangland conflict that began in the late 1920s and ended in 1931] no internal squabbles married the unity of our Family and no outside interference threatened the Family or me.

Part of the reason for this was that for many years, the FBI ignored the activities of organized crime families. FBI director J. Edgar Hoover often denied that there was any national network of criminals.

By the late 1950s, however, the Commission system was beginning to unravel. In 1957, police raided a meeting of about 100 mob leaders in the small town of Apalachin, New York. The mobsters fled, but nearly 60 were captured. Some were convicted of minor charges, though the convictions were all overturned on appeal. Nevertheless, the arrests had far-reaching consequences, indicating that criminal groups from across the nation did work together.

In 1963 a soldier in the Genovese crime family of New York, Joseph Valachi, became the first mobster to speak publicly about organized crime, breaking the mob code of silence, or *omerta*. He testified before a U.S. Senate committee about the existence of the Italian mafia, which he called *la cosa nostra* (Italian for "our thing.") Faced with clear evidence that he had been mistaken, Hoover finally began devoting FBI resources to combat organized crime.

Throughout the rest of the 1960s state and federal law enforcement officials made many arrests. However, most of those arrested and convicted were low-level associates of the crime families that worked as bookmakers, pimps, and enforcers. The structure of crime families meant that the bosses were largely protected from prosecution. The bosses did not commit the criminal acts, they ordered their underbosses to arrange for others to do the crimes. Therefore, the only person who could link a mob boss to a crime was one of his trusted underbosses, who were highly unlikely to break the *omerta* code.

The task of putting high-ranking

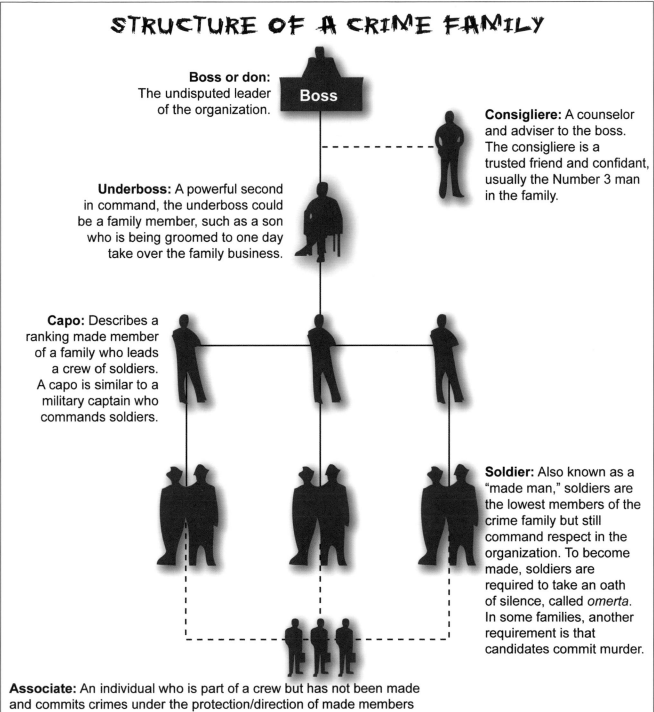

STRUCTURE OF A CRIME FAMILY

Boss or don: The undisputed leader of the organization.

Boss

Consigliere: A counselor and adviser to the boss. The consigliere is a trusted friend and confidant, usually the Number 3 man in the family.

Underboss: A powerful second in command, the underboss could be a family member, such as a son who is being groomed to one day take over the family business.

Capo: Describes a ranking made member of a family who leads a crew of soldiers. A capo is similar to a military captain who commands soldiers.

Soldier: Also known as a "made man," soldiers are the lowest members of the crime family but still command respect in the organization. To become made, soldiers are required to take an oath of silence, called *omerta*. In some families, another requirement is that candidates commit murder.

Associate: An individual who is part of a crew but has not been made and commits crimes under the protection/direction of made members and remits a share of his illegal proceeds to his direct made superior.

Organized crime bosses come from many ethnic backgrounds. (Left) Irish-American James "Whitey" Bulger ran the most powerful mob in Boston for decades. He was finally captured in 2011 and charged with dozens of RICO Act violations—including 19 murders. (Right) Eduardo Ravelo is a capo in a Mexican-American criminal organization called Barrio Azteca. He is on the FBI's "Most Wanted" list for drug trafficking, money laundering, and other racketeering activities.

mobsters behind bars became easier with the passage of the Racketeer Influenced and Corrupt Organizations (RICO) Act in 1970. This federal law specifies nearly three dozen specific racketeering-related crimes. Most importantly, it allows the leader of an organization such as a crime family to be tried for an activity that he ordered an underling to do. This meant that a mob boss who ordered an enemy to be killed could be tried for the murder as though he had committed it.

Employing the RICO laws, as well as wiretaps and regular surveillance of known or suspected gang members, over the past four decades prosecutors have succeeded in jailing many mobsters. During the 1990s, the arrest of hundreds of mobsters and the conviction of mob bosses like John Gotti, head of the Gambino crime family, and Vincent "Chin" Gigante, head of the Genovese family, indicated that the Italian-American mob was in decline. Yet the FBI still considers it to be "the foremost organized criminal threat to American society," with an annual revenue of more than $100 billion.

In recent years, other gangs have become involved in organized criminal activity in the United States. These include Russian mobsters who came to the United States after the collapse of the Soviet Union; groups from African countries like Nigeria that engage in drug trafficking and financial scams; Asian criminal organizations like the Japanese Yazuka and Chinese Tongs; and groups from Mexico and South America that are engaged in drug trafficking and other illicit activities. An FBI report notes:

> All of these groups have a presence in the U.S. or are targeting our citizens from afar—using the Internet and other technologies of our global age. More and more, they are literally becoming partners in crime, realizing they have more to gain from cooperating than competing.

Criminals have always been able to adapt to changing social and political conditions. The crime families of today are likely to survive, and thrive, for a long time.

JOHNNY TORRIO
THE CHICAGO FOX

During the early years of the 20th century, there were three major criminal figures who shared the same nickname—"the Brain." They were Meyer Lansky, Arnold Rothstein, and Johnny Torrio. While all three men were willing to use violence when necessary, they shared a vision greater than bullets, bootlegging, and bookmaking. They wanted to organize criminal activities on a national level and run gangs in similar fashion to legitimate corporations.

Johnny Torrio was the first of these three innovative mobsters. He played a pivotal role in establishing a link between the original street gangs of New York, which were based on ethnic and territorial divisions, and the newer ones that would arise around the time of the Prohibition era. Torrio created the foundation for the American mafia, the network of crime families that exist today.

Torrio was born in Italy in 1882. Two years later he emigrated from Italy to New York with his recently widowed mother. When he was in his early teens, he joined a street gang in Lower Manhattan called the James Streeters. He soon became the gang's leader, and made enough money to open a pool hall, which the gang used as a headquarters for its illegal activities. These included gambling, prostitution, and selling drugs.

Even though he was a short man, Torrio gained a reputation for being able to take care of himself in fights, no matter what the weapon. He soon came to the attention of another Italian immigrant, Paolo Antonini Vaccarelli, who was better known as Paul Kelly. Kelly was in charge of Lower Manhattan's most powerful criminal organization in the 1890s, the Five Points Gang. He brought Torrio into his organization

A view of South Water Street, Chicago, in 1915, the year that Brooklyn gangster Johnny Torrio moved permanently to the city to work with "Big Jim" Colosimo.

around 1900, and served as a mentor to the younger criminal, teaching him how to dress like a gentleman and to present himself as a young businessman. Torrio eventually became Kelly's second-in-command. In addition to illegal activities, Torrio also ran several legitimate saloons and his pool hall. He and a good friend from the Five Points Gang, Frankie Yale, owned the Harvard Inn on Coney Island. Among the people they employed there was a teenage hoodlum named Alphonse "Al" Capone.

In 1909 Torrio received a message from Giacomo "Big Jim" Colosimo, who ran a criminal organization in Chicago. He had been threatened by some Italian gangsters as part of an extortion racket.

Colosimo was married to one of Torrio's cousins, who had suggested that he could help. Torrio came to Chicago and soon arranged for the extortionists to be killed.

Over the next few years, Torrio returned to Chicago several times to do other "favors" for Colosimo. In 1915, Colosimo offered him a full-time job running the day-to-day operations of his illegal businesses. Torrio turned control of his New York operations over to Frankie Yale and moved to Chicago. There, he helped to build the Colosimo outfit into one of Chicago's most powerful gangs. The gang made most of its money from prostitution, running a number of brothels in the city's South Side.

In 1918, when the 19-year-old Capone got into trouble with gangsters in Brooklyn, Yale set him to Chicago to join Colosimo's outfit. Capone proved to be an ideal fit for Torrio and quickly became his most trusted assistant.

By this time, it was clear that Prohibition would soon become federal law. Torrio recognized that huge profits could be made by supplying illegal alcohol. There was just one problem—thanks to Torrio's handling, Colosimo's businesses had become so profitable that the mob boss did not want to branch out into bootlegging.

Torrio was ambitious and confident. He decided that Colosimo had to be eliminated. (By this time Colosimo had abandoned Torrio's cousin and married another woman.) On May 11, 1920, Colosimo was killed when he visited a warehouse. No one was ever arrested for the murder, although most people believe Torrio had arranged the hit with Frankie Yale and that Capone had also been involved.

With Colosimo out of the picture, Torrio took over the South Side organization. His first order of business was an effort to bring all the major Chicago gangs into a single confederation, in which each gang would have its own area of power and influence. He felt confident that he could buy off local politicians and police, thereby enabling all of the gangs to flourish and maxi-

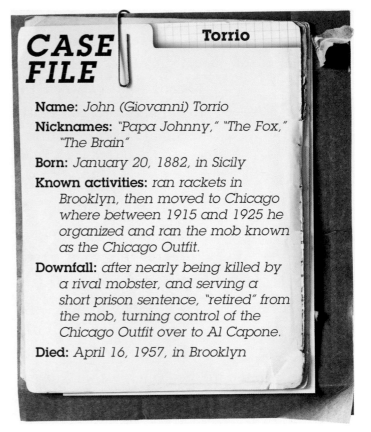

CASE FILE   Torrio

Name: *John (Giovanni) Torrio*

Nicknames: *"Papa Johnny," "The Fox," "The Brain"*

Born: *January 20, 1882, in Sicily*

Known activities: *ran rackets in Brooklyn, then moved to Chicago where between 1915 and 1925 he organized and ran the mob known as the Chicago Outfit.*

Downfall: *after nearly being killed by a rival mobster, and serving a short prison sentence, "retired" from the mob, turning control of the Chicago Outfit over to Al Capone.*

Died: *April 16, 1957, in Brooklyn*

mize their profits without fear of conflict with other gangs.

The plan worked well for several years, but some of the gangsters gradually became dissatisfied. Among them was Dion O'Banion, a ruthless Irish-American killer who was the leader of Chicago's North Side Gang. O'Banion began to push for a larger share of the bootlegging revenue. Torrio wanted to keep peace, so he gave in to some of O'Banion's demands.

However, Torrio refused to intervene when O'Banion complained that the Genna crime family, which was run by six Italian-American brothers and based in Chicago's Little Italy neighborhood, was trying to sell its bootleg alcohol in the North Side. Frustrated, O'Banion began hijacking the Genna gang's shipments of illegal alcohol. A low-level gang war between the Gennas and the North Side Gang erupted.

Dion O'Banion

Tensions came to a head in 1924, after O'Banion offered to sell Torrio his share in a secret brewing operation for $500,000 (the equivalent of more than $6 million in 2013 dollars). O'Banion claimed he wanted to get out of the Chicago rackets and move to Colorado, and Torrio jumped at the chance to rid his city of a rival. Shortly after turning over the money, the brewery was raided by federal agents, who arrested Torrio and charged him with violating the Volstead Act. Torrio, who was sentenced to nine months in prison, was angry when he learned that O'Banion had known before making the deal that the brewery was going to be raided and had let Torrio take the fall. He arranged for the North Side gangster to be killed by his Brooklyn associate Frankie Yale and two other hit men.

Frankie Yale

O'Banion was assassinated in the flower store that he owned on November 10, 1924.

The murder touched off a bloody gang war in Chicago between the North Side Gang and its allies, who were mostly Irish or Jewish gangsters, and the Italian crime families of Chicago. The war would last for years, finally winding down after the infamous St. Valentine's Day Massacre of seven North Side Gang members in February 1929.

By that time Torrio was no longer involved with the South Side gang. He had known that the killing of O'Banion would prompt retaliation, and it came quickly. On January 24, 1925, three members of the North Side Gang—Hymie Weiss, Vincent Drucci, and George "Bugs" Moran—ambushed Torrio as he was returning home from a shopping trip. Weiss, who had taken over as gang leader after O'Banion's death, blasted Torrio with a shotgun. Moran had also hit the Italian gangster with several shots. As he prepared to fire a fatal bullet into Torrio's head, Moran realized that his handgun was empty. The North Side gunmen fled, leaving

Hymie Weiss

Torrio bleeding from numerous wounds.

Miraculously, Torrio survived after more than a week of intensive care. A few weeks later, he began serving his jail term, though his friendship with the sheriff guaranteed that it was as comfortable as possible.

Not surprisingly, Torrio did some serious thinking. His hopes of controlling Chicago had collapsed, and he knew that if he stayed in the city he would be a marked man. Now in his early 40s, he had an estimated $30 million hidden away. Torrio decided it was time to step down. He turned control of his empire over to Capone, and moved to Italy, where he lived for several years.

After returning to the United States in the early 1930s, Torrio settled in Brooklyn and led a quiet life selling real estate. Though he refused to become actively involved in any further illegal activity, many of the new generation of crime bosses came to him for advice. Torrio said his only goal was to die in bed.

He almost got his wish. While getting a haircut in April 1957, Torrio suffered a heart attack. He stayed alive just long enough to be taken to a hospital, where he died. By then the man who at one time had been regarded as Public

Johnny Torrio in New York during 1939. During this time the "retired" gangster often dispensed advice to the younger generation of mob leaders.

Enemy No. 1 had become almost totally forgotten. It was three weeks after his burial that the media even took notice.

Al Capone winks at a photographer while walking down the steps of a courthouse, 1930s. Capone was one of the most ruthless gangsters of the Prohibition era; he is believed to have committed several murders, and ordered the killings of hundreds of rival gang members during the time he ran the infamous Chicago Outfit.

AL CAPONE
BRUTAL KING OF CHICAGO

In the public imagination, no one is more closely associated with organized crime than Al Capone. During his rise to gangland fame and fortune, Capone underwent a stunning transformation—from a teenage petty thug to a sophisticated businessman who controlled much of the political structure of Chicago by the time he was in his mid-20s.

One of the primary reasons for his notoriety was the media attention Capone constantly received. Unlike most mobsters, who preferred to stay out of the limelight, Capone was a publicity hound who loved being in the spotlight. "He was a gabber," explains Capone biographer Jonathan Eig. "He was such a gregarious guy that when the reporters came around, he just wouldn't shut up. So he became a celebrity, and he really believed he could get away with it. . . . Only during Prohibition could somebody doing this work begin to think of themselves as being high-class and having a high profile. That's really the key for Capone, and that's why we're so fascinated with him today. He wasn't shy about his illegal activities. He bragged about them."

Yet Capone's time at the top lasted for just a few years. His fall was almost as swift as his rise. He spent the final years of his life wracked with disease and pain.

Born in Brooklyn, New York, on January 17, 1899, Alphonse Gabriel Capone was the fourth child of Gabriele and Theresina Capone, who had come to the United States from their native Italy five years earlier. Gabriele worked in a grocery store when he arrived and saved enough money to start his own barber shop. Young Al grew up in relative comfort. But when he was 14, he slapped a teacher and was kicked out of

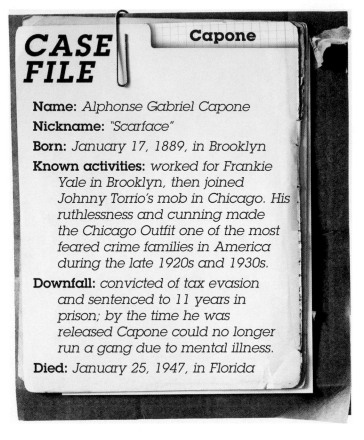

CASE FILE

Capone

Name: *Alphonse Gabriel Capone*

Nickname: *"Scarface"*

Born: *January 17, 1889, in Brooklyn*

Known activities: *worked for Frankie Yale in Brooklyn, then joined Johnny Torrio's mob in Chicago. His ruthlessness and cunning made the Chicago Outfit one of the most feared crime families in America during the late 1920s and 1930s.*

Downfall: *convicted of tax evasion and sentenced to 11 years in prison; by the time he was released Capone could no longer run a gang due to mental illness.*

Died: *January 25, 1947, in Florida*

school. He began hanging out with members of the local gangs. Soon he began working as a bartender and enforcer for Brooklyn mobster Frankie Yale, who controlled most of the area's criminal activities.

One night in 1917, Capone was working at a nightclub owned by Yale when he made a pass at a girl whose brother was Frank Galluccio, a small-time hoodlum. Galluccio pulled out a knife and sliced the left side of Capone's face three times. The wounds required several dozen stitches to close. The scars that resulted gave Capone his life-long nickname, "Scarface."

Even as a teenager, Capone had a reputation as a ruthless enforcer. One

night in 1918 Yale sent Capone to collect money a gambler owed to him. When the man refused to pay the debt, even though he had the money, Capone beat him savagely, then shot him to death. Such brutal methods meant that Capone drew the attention of New York police. To protect his young protege from a murder investigation, in 1919 Yale sent Capone to Chicago, where he could work for Johnny Torrio.

The timing proved to be ideal. When Prohibition began in 1920—by coincidence, it was the day that Al Capone turned 21—he was a small fish, just one of Johnny Torrio's many employees. But he quickly made himself indispensable to Torrio. The older gangster returned the favor by teaching Capone "the importance of leading an outwardly respectable life, to segregate his career from his home life, as if maintaining a peaceful, conventional domestic setting somehow excused or legitimized the venality of working in the rackets," notes biographer, Laurence Bergreen. "It was a form of hypocrisy that was second nature to Johnny Torrio and that he taught Capone to honor."

Torrio had foreseen the immense sums to be made during Prohibition. Coupled with their other criminal enterprises in Chicago, by 1925 both men were extremely wealthy. At that point, Torrio was nearly killed by members of the rival North Side Gang. He soon "retired" to Italy, leaving Capone in charge of their so-called Chicago Outfit.

Although the Chicago Outfit earned millions through bootlegging, prostitution, and gambling, Capone didn't think of himself as a criminal. In his view he was simply an ambitious man taking advantage of the American system, which rewarded hard work and individual enterprise. He once explained:

> I make my money by supplying a public demand. If I break the law, my customers, who number hundreds of the best people in Chicago, are as guilty as I am. The only difference between us is that I sell and they buy. Everybody calls me a racketeer. I call myself a business man. When I sell liquor, it's bootlegging. When my patrons serve it on a silver tray on Lake Shore Drive, it's hospitality."

Alluding to the failed attempts of many other Italian Americans to enter "respectable" occupations, Capone

This portrait of Capone shows the distinctive scars on his left cheek. The gangster would later hire Frank Galluccio, the man who had knifed him, as a bodyguard.

added, "Why, I tried to get into legitimate businesses two or three times, but they won't stand for it."

In the media, Capone portrayed himself as an hard-working family man. He and his wife, Mae, lived in a modest house on South Prairie Avenue in Chicago with their son Albert "Sonny" Capone. He received good publicity for making generous donations to children's charities and providing financial help to local widows.

Al Capone portrayed himself as a type of Robin Hood who shared his wealth with people who were less fortunate. These men are standing outside a soup kitchen he opened for the unemployed in Chicago during the early years of the Great Depression.

The bodies of dead gangsters lie on the floor of a Chicago warehouse following the St. Valentine's Day massacre, February 14, 1929. Although in the short term the attack rid Capone of some North Side enemies, the massacre damaged his carefully cultivated public image. Americans began to view Capone as a brutal killer, and began to insist that police do more to prevent gang violence.

Capone was generous with his wealth when it came to local authorities. He bribed policemen, building inspectors, judges, and other officials to ignore his gang's criminal activities. Capone's control over civic authorities in Cook County—in which Chicago is located—was so complete that many people referred to him as "the mayor of Crook County."

Yet in the ruthless criminal underworld of Chicago, Capone frequently found himself in the crosshairs of other gangs. The bloody war between his outfit and the North Side Gang had continued. One of the worst attempts on his life came in 1926 when 10 cars pulled up outside a restaurant where Capone was eating. Several men armed with Thompson submachine guns leaped out of each car and sprayed the building with gunfire before speeding away. Miraculously, no one was killed, and Capone paid for medical care for several bystanders who had been injured in the attack.

In 1929, Capone's men struck back at the North Side Gang. Several of Capone's shooters dressed up as police officers and "arrested" a group of North Side gangsters who were at a warehouse to pick up a shipment of illegal liquor. Capone had hoped to capture George "Bugs" Moran, but the North Side Gang leader had seen the police cars on his way to the warehouse and turned around. It was a wise decision for Moran. Without warning, the "cops" opened fire on the unfortunate North Side gangsters. Seven were killed, some nearly cut in half by machine-gun bullets. Because the incident happened on February 14, the gruesome killings were promptly christened the St. Valentine's Day Massacre.

Capone had not been at the massacre—he was at an estate in Florida at the time—and claimed that he had nothing to do with it. However, no one believed him. "Only Capone kills like that," Bugs Moran told police. Soon, though, Capone would take a personal hand in another brutal act of violence. The gang leader demanded loyalty from those who worked for him. In May 1929 he learned that three of his top hitmen had spoken with a rival mobster about betraying Capone. Pretending not to know anything about the plot, Capone invited the three men to a special dinner. While there, Capone beat the men with a bat and had them murdered.

Incidents like these began to change the public's perception of Al Capone from a celebrity businessman to a cold-blooded killer. Across the nation, the rise in gangland violence had resulted in calls to crack down on organized crime. Under pressure from the public, Chicago police started to crack down on illegal activities. The federal government also began investigating Capone and other gangsters for Prohibition-related crimes.

In August 1929, Capone and his bodyguard were arrested in Philadelphia and charged with carrying concealed weapons. He was convicted and spent nine months behind bars. It was the first time in his long and bloody career that Capone had done prison time.

By the time he was released, two federal investigations were well underway. The Department of the Treasury, which had jurisdiction in Prohibition-related cases, had sent an agent named Eliot Ness to raid Capone's illegal breweries and disrupt his bootlegging operations. Ness was in charge of a group of trustworthy agents;

Eliot Ness

Capone's failed attempt to bribe them led to the group being nicknamed "the Untouchables." During a six-month period the Untouchables seized millions in illegal liquor and brewing equipment, and arrested many of Capone's distributors. This in turn deprived the gangster of revenue he needed to keep the bribes flowing to Chicago police and politicians.

At the same time, the Internal Revenue Service had sent an agent named Frank J. Wilson to investigate Capone's finances. A few years earlier, the U.S. Supreme Court

Frank J. Wilson

The jury verdict in Al Capone's trial, signed by jurors on October 17, 1931. The gangster was found guilty on five of the 22 charges.

On October 6, 1931, Al Capone's trial began in Chicago. At the start of the trial, Judge James H. Wilkerson told the court bailiff to take the jury down the hall to another judge's court, and to bring the jury which had been selected for that trial to his courtroom. The move shocked Capone, whose men had learned the identities of jurors and bribed them to acquit their boss. Switching the juries would ensure that Capone would receive a fair trial. During the trial, the judge made sure that jurors were kept away from possible interference by Capone's men.

During the trial, the government tried to show that Capone had not paid taxes on the millions of dollars he earned from bootlegging and other criminal activities. Some of the gangster's former bookkeepers testified against him. Chicago newspapers printed several editions every day so the public could stay abreast of the latest developments.

On October 17, 1931, the jury found Capone guilty on five of the government's charges. A week later, Judge Wilkerson sentenced the 32-year-old Capone to 11 years in federal prison and ordered him to pay fines and court costs of more than $80,000. He was also ordered to pay $215,000 in back taxes.

Capone began serving his sentence at a federal prison in Atlanta, Georgia,

had ruled that money earned illegally was still subject to income tax. Capone had carefully hidden his illegal income, but an exhaustive examination by federal auditors produced enough evidence for a trial. The gangster was charged with 22 counts of income tax evasion.

Al Capone was inmate number 85 at Alcactraz, a federal prison established to hold America's most dangerous criminals. Capone's health deteriorated during the six years he spent at Alcatraz.

in 1932. He was able to sneak money into the prison, which he used to bribe guards for special privileges. Capone was also able to communicate with his underworld associates from prison.

Things changed in 1934, when Capone was transferred to the newly established high-security federal penitentiary on Alcatraz Island in San Francisco Bay. At Alcatraz, Capone was rarely permitted to have visitors, and they could only be close family members. There was no way to smuggle money to Capone, or to deliver his messages to former confederates. He had no access to newspapers, so he could not follow things that were going on in Chicago or elsewhere.

At Alcatraz, Capone soon learned that his reputation didn't mean much. Early in his stay he tried to cut to the front of a line for a haircut. James Lucas, a Texan serving a sentence for bank robbery, told him to get back. "Do you know who I am, punk?" Capone snarled. Lucas grabbed a pair of scissors, stuck the point into Capone's neck, and repeated his earlier command. Capone complied.

Although Capone adjusted to prison, his health deteriorated. As a young man he had been infected with syphilis, a

Wearing a bathrobe, Al Capone fishes from the deck of a boat near his Miami estate, 1940s. After his release from prison the once-feared gangster was no longer able to run a crime family due to the disease that destroyed his sanity.

sexually transmitted disease. If it is not treated, syphilis can affect the brain and central nervous system many years after the original infection. This is what happened in Capone's case. By the late 1930s he was disoriented and could no longer think clearly. His speech was slurred, his walk a slow shuffle. In 1939 his close friend, the Chicago Outfit's financial and legal advisor Jake "Greasy Thumb" Guzik, commented on the state of Capone's mind: "Al? He's as nutty as a fruitcake."

That year, Capone was released on parole due to his failing mental and physical health. He moved to Florida, where he lived with his wife Mae and his mother at an estate in Miami. His health continued to fail. In 1946, his doctor reported that Capone had the mental ability of a 12-year-old boy.

In January 1947 the gangster suffered a stroke. A few days later, on January 25, 1947, Capone died of heart failure at age 48.

ARNOLD ROTHSTEIN
THE BUSINESS OF CRIME

Many gangsters who flourished during the Prohibition era came from impoverished backgrounds. They started out as small-time criminals and gradually scratched and fought their way up to become gang leaders. This was not the case for Arnold Rothstein, born in 1882 to a well-to-do family in New York City.

Arnold's father, Abraham Rothstein, was a prominent Jewish businessman in New York. Abraham was highly respected because of his philanthropy and his reputation for honest business dealings. In 1919, New York governor Al Smith even referred to Abraham Rothstein as "Abe the Just" after he helped to settle a labor strike. One of Arnold Rothstein's brothers became a Jewish rabbi, or religious leader. Abraham Rothstein undoubtedly hoped that his younger son Arnold would also make his mark in a respectable way.

Despite having a stable home life and learning early lessons in graceful social interaction, Arnold would not fulfill his father's hopes for his future. Instead, by the early 1900s Rothstein had made crime his business, forever changing the way that organized criminals would operate. Historian and author Robert Rockaway notes:

> Rothstein is recognized as the pioneer "big businessman" of organized crime in the United States. A man of prodigious energy, imagination and intellect, he transformed American crime from petty larceny into big business. One social historian described him as "the J.P. Morgan of the underworld; its banker and master of strategy."

Notorious gangster Meyer Lansky, one of Rothstein's protégés who later adopted the same businesslike approach to criminal activity, would later say that Rothstein was so smart

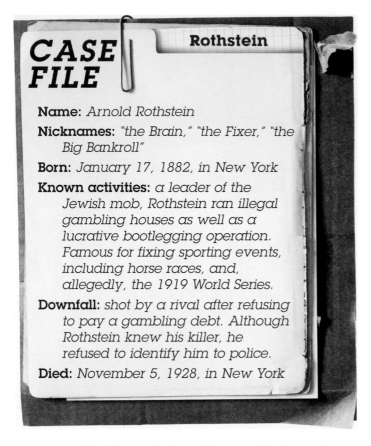

CASE FILE

Rothstein

Name: *Arnold Rothstein*

Nicknames: *"the Brain," "the Fixer," "the Big Bankroll"*

Born: *January 17, 1882, in New York*

Known activities: *a leader of the Jewish mob, Rothstein ran illegal gambling houses as well as a lucrative bootlegging operation. Famous for fixing sporting events, including horse races, and, allegedly, the 1919 World Series.*

Downfall: *shot by a rival after refusing to pay a gambling debt. Although Rothstein knew his killer, he refused to identify him to police.*

Died: *November 5, 1928, in New York*

From an early age, Rothstein staked out his own path in life. He had little interest in school, preferring instead to play cards and throw dice with his friends. He fell behind, eventually dropping two grades and winding up in the same class as his younger brother Edgar. "I'd do all the homework and Arnold would copy it and remember it. Except in arithmetic. Arnold did all the arithmetic. He loved to play with numbers," Edgar recalled. Rothstein parlayed his love of numbers into a method of calculating the odds in gambling.

This method became especially useful when he dropped out of school at the age of 16. He became increasingly successful in gambling houses and pool halls, making enough money to begin a career as a "loan shark," a person who loans money at very high interest rates. When a person borrows money from a

and talented that he could have been just as successful financially if he had been involved in legitimate business rather than in crime.

Young paperboys play craps, a gambling game with dice, in a New York alley, circa 1910. Rothstein used his own gambling winnings to build a successful business financing other gamblers with loans, and eventually opening his own casinos.

loan shark and loses it gambling, the interest rates are often so high that it becomes very difficult for that person to pay back the loan.

Any time Rothstein had a problem collecting the money he was owed, he would turn to hired thugs, who would threaten or beat up debtors until they repaid. This was the start of a lifelong practice. Rothstein was always careful to limit his personal exposure in such matters. He preferred to let others get their hands dirty. "Known along Broadway as 'the Brain' and 'the Big Bankroll,' Rothstein was an unthreatening-looking figure, soft-spoken, and a spiffy dresser," notes author Selwyn Raab. "His authority was enforced by an entourage of brutal henchmen."

The "Big Bankroll" nickname referred to another practice by Rothstein. He carried a large wad of cash with him at all times. "Money talks," Rothstein once explained. "The more money, the louder it talks."

From an early age, Rothstein understood a central truth of gambling: it is more profitable to be the gambling house than the gambler who is a guest of that house. In games of chance, the odds are generally tilted in the house's favor. In 1909, Rothstein opened a casino in Manhattan. It was the first of what became a string of high-class casinos throughout the New York area.

Rothstein also purchased racehorses and invested in racetracks. He sometimes secretly collaborated with jockeys and trainers to make sure that a certain horse would win. This is known as "fixing a race." Rothstein would then place a large bet on the sure winner, and would pocket a huge profit.

With so much money rolling in, Rothstein invested some by paying bribes to policemen and New York politicians so they would not interfere with his illegal business activities. The

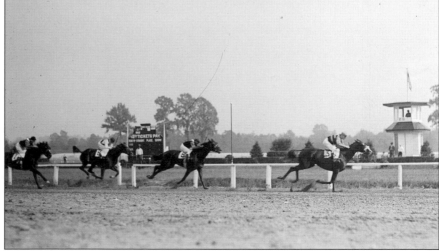

The finish of a 1919 race at Laurel, Maryland, one of the tracks where Rothstein enjoyed betting on horse races. Rothstein won tens of thousands of dollars betting on horses, including $450,000 in winning tickets on his horse Sporting Blood in the 1920 Travers Stakes at Saratoga Springs, New York.

During the early 1920s one of the regulars in Arnold Rothstein's gambling houses was a young writer named F. Scott Fitzgerald, best-known today for his novel *The Great Gatsby*. When writing that novel, Fitzgerald (pictured here in 1925 with his wife Zelda) used Rothstein as a model for his character Meyer Wolfsheim, who helps Jay Gatsby mysteriously amass a vast fortune. Some scholars believe that some parts of the fictional Gatsby's elegant, suave personality were also based on Rothstein.

network of political and police contacts that he developed enabled him to avoid criminal charges and protected his associates. In exchange, he used gang members to make sure that candidates he supported for local offices would be elected. The gambling kingpin became known as "the Fixer," in part because of his gambling background but also because it seemed he could get local government officials to do practically anything he wanted.

Rothstein's fortune became even larger once the Prohibition era began in 1920. He was among the first underworld figures to recognize the immense amounts of money that could be made by providing a product, alcohol, that was in great demand because it was illegal. He soon financed a bootlegging operation, recruiting members of Jewish and Italian street gangs in New York to distribute the illegal liquor. Among them were Charles "Lucky" Luciano and Waxey Gordon, a Philadelphia mob boss who ran the operation. Some of the other gang members who would go on to infamous gangland careers after working in Rothstein's criminal organization included Frank Costello, Jack "Legs" Diamond, Meyer Lansky, and Dutch Schultz.

Many of these former street thugs would later credit Rothstein with helping them to create a veneer of respectability that they would use as they became top members of the underworld during the 1920s and 1930s. "[Rothstein] taught me how to dress . . . how to use knives and forks and things like that at the dinner table, about holdin' a door open for a girl," Luciano would later say. "If Arnold had lived a little longer, he could've made me pretty elegant."

Waxey Gordon

Within a few years, it became apparent to Rothstein that bootlegging was far too big and decentralized for one person—even one with the political contacts that he had—to control. He decided to move into another area, narcotics. At that time much of the clientele consisted of wealthy people and movie stars who could easily afford to pay for drugs.

Rothstein also used his hired muscle to become involved in labor unions. Workers in New York's garment industry who were on strike for better wages and working conditions paid Rothstein's organization for guards that would protect them from "strike-breakers" hired by the factory owners to attack the workers. Unknown to the workers, Rothstein also contracted with industrialists to provide thugs as strike-breakers. His underlings Louis "Lepke" Buchalter and Jacob "Gurrah" Shapiro eventually gained control of the unions, and the New York garment industry, through force and fear.

For unknown reasons, Rothstein's health suffered a decline during 1928. His eyes and hands often twitched uncontrollably and his speech was frequently slurred even though he didn't drink. At the same time, he began an extended losing streak in which for the first time ever he lost consistently in card games, his racehorses finished well out of the money, and his gambling establishments were raided by police.

Arnold Rothstein exits a car during a visit to Chicago.

In early September of 1928, Rothstein participated in a marathon poker game at the Park Central Hotel that spanned three days. Rothstein was hoping to recover some of the money he had lost during the year. This wasn't an unrealistic expectation, considering that

Rothstein's most infamous coup was his involvement in fixing the 1919 World Series between the Chicago White Sox and Cincinnati Reds. Eight members of the heavily favored White Sox agreed to lose the games on purpose so that gamblers could win big betting on the Reds. When the plot was uncovered in 1920, it caused a national scandal.

three years earlier he'd won $604,000 in a single hand of poker from the noted professional gambler Nick "the Greek" Dandalos when the final card gave him a flush. Things didn't work out as well this time, however. Rothstein's run of bad luck continued and he lost more than $320,000 in the game.

The fact that Rothstein had lost so much money sent shock waves through the New York underworld. It was even more shocking that Rothstein refused to pay the debt. He claimed that the game had been fixed, and ignored several "suggestions" that he pay up.

Nearly two months after the game,

on November 2, 1928, Rothstein was invited to the Park Central for another poker game with George "Hump" McManus, a well-known New York bookmaker. Later that evening, a hotel employee found Rothstein in a hallway with a bullet wound in his stomach. Even though Rothstein almost certainly knew the identity of the shooter, he remained true to the underworld code of silence. A detective who interviewed Rothstein as he lay dying the next day later told reporters that the gambling kingpin had said, "I'm not talking to you. You stick to your trade, I'll stick to mine."

Hump McManus, who had also been at the original card game with Rothstein at the Park Central, was arrested in connection with the crime. Most experts believe that McManus probably shot Rothstein in a drunken rage because he was angry about the debt. However, there was not enough evidence to convict him. Rothstein's underlings, particularly Luciano and Meyer Lansky, took control of his criminal activities and continued them into the 1930s.

Today, nearly a century after his death, Arnold Rothstein has largely been forgotten. When he is remembered, it is often for his connection with the "Black Sox scandal." In 1919, several members of the Chicago White Sox baseball team agreed to a plot developed by some gamblers to lose the World Series on purpose. Rothstein is believed to have helped to finance the World Series fix, then bet heavily on the team's opponent, the Cincinnati Reds, knowing that they would win.

The White Sox were the best team in baseball, which at the time was the most popular sport in America. They had won the previous World Series, and many people were betting on them to win again in 1919. When the White Sox lost the World Series to the Reds, it was a huge upset. Gamblers who had bet on the underdog Reds made a lot of money.

When news began to emerge about the connection between ballplayers and gamblers in 1920, it resulted in a criminal investigation. Eight members of the White Sox were eventually linked to the plot to fix the Series. Although all eight men were acquitted at a trial in 1921, they were banned from playing professional baseball forever. One of them was "Shoeless" Joe Jackson, who is considered one of the best hitters of all time.

The grand jury that investigated the scandal could not find enough evidence to indict Rothstein. His bodyguard, Abe Attell, was charged with developing the plot, but like the ballplayers he was acquitted. As with the circumstances of Rothstein's 1928 murder, the truth of the infamous gambler's involvement in the Black Sox scandal is likely to remain forever shrouded in mystery.

CHARLES "LUCKY" LUCIANO
CRIMINAL MASTERMIND

In 1998 *Time* magazine published a list of the 100 most important people of the 20th century. Albert Einstein, headed the list, followed by people like Walt Disney, Henry Ford, Adolf Hitler, Winston Churchill, and Oprah Winfrey.

Of course, few people agreed with all of *Time*'s selections. But no person on the magazine's list elicited more criticism than Charles "Lucky" Luciano, whose occupation writer Edna Buchanan noted as "criminal mastermind." Buchanan explained:

> The FBI describes Luciano's ascendancy as the watershed event in the history of organized crime. . . . Luciano organized organized crime. He modernized the Mafia, shaping it into a smoothly run national crime syndicate focused on the bottom line.

Born Salvatore Lucania in 1897 in Sicily, the boy came to the United States with his family when he was nine. Because he could barely speak English, school had no appeal to him. What did appeal to him was getting paid to provide "protection" to scrawny Jewish youngsters who did want to go to school but were often preyed upon by street gangs. For a penny or two, Luciano would escort them safely to school. If they refused, he often beat them up.

Later, Luciana went to work at a hat factory, where the $7 weekly salary had little appeal. According to the *New York Times*, "After winning $244 in a craps game, he never did another honest day's work. 'Who wants to wind up being a crumb?' he remarked to a friend. 'I'd rather drop dead.'"

Soon no one would dare consider Lucky Luciano a "crumb"—1920s slang for a worthless person. He began working for Five Points Gang boss Frankie Yale, then was hired as a gunman by another New York City mobster, Giuseppe "Joe the Boss" Masseria.

Masseria was a "Mustache Pete"—an immigrant who had been connected with the Sicilian Mafia, an organization of gangs that ran illegal activities in Sicily. The Mustache Petes who came to America were interested in continuing their traditional activities—protection rackets, kidnappings for ransom, and robberies. They were suspicious about new ways to make money, such as through selling drugs or bootlegging alcohol, and refused to work with Jewish, Irish, and even non-Sicilian Italian gangsters in these non-traditional but highly lucrative activities.

Luciano, although a Sicilian, was willing to work with anyone so long as he could make money at it. In 1921 he left Masseria's organization and began working in a bootlegging operation that Arnold Rothstein—the dominant figure in New York's organized crime scene at that time—helped to plan and finance. Luciano worked with several Jewish gangsters that he had known for many years, including Meyer Lansky and Ben "Bugsy" Siegel. Bootlegging was highly profitable, and Luciano soon branched out into other areas, primarily drug distribution and prostitution. By the mid-1920s Luciano was earning millions of dollars each year.

It was about this time that Luciano acquired his enduring nickname of

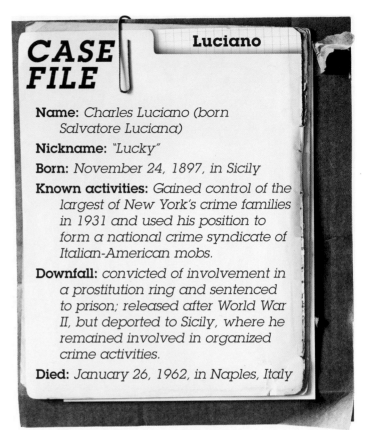

CASE FILE   Luciano

Name: *Charles Luciano (born Salvatore Luciana)*

Nickname: *"Lucky"*

Born: *November 24, 1897, in Sicily*

Known activities: *Gained control of the largest of New York's crime families in 1931 and used his position to form a national crime syndicate of Italian-American mobs.*

Downfall: *convicted of involvement in a prostitution ring and sentenced to prison; released after World War II, but deported to Sicily, where he remained involved in organized crime activities.*

Died: *January 26, 1962, in Naples, Italy*

"Lucky." It's not clear how he got the name. It might have been from gambling successes, or from mispronunciation of his last name. (Apparently, Jewish immigrants had such a hard time saying "Salvatore Luciana" that he changed his name to "Charles Luciano.") It could have been because he was often arrested but rarely served prison time. Some gangsters said that Luciano got the name because he survived several attempts on his life, including one savage beating in 1929 when he was strung up in a warehouse and tortured with knives and clubs. His attackers dumped him on a beach in Staten Island. Somehow he survived,

Police investigate a bullet-riddled taxi, with the bodies of two gangsters lying in the street nearby, during the 1931 Castellammarese War.

Charles Luciano mugshot, taken by New York police in 1931.

though one eyelid had a permanent droop and he was left with a prominent scar on his chin.

When Rothstein was killed in 1928, Luciano rejoined Masseria's organization. By that time New York's crime scene had been complicated by the arrival of another Sicilian mobster, Salvatore Maranzano. Soon the two Mafia leaders engaged in a bloody struggle for control of the New York underworld. In the so-called Castellammarese War of 1931, gunmen from both gangs disrupted each others' rackets and often killed each other. The war lasted for several years.

The Castellammarese War was bad for the business of crime. Luciano and other young mobsters who worked with Masseria's organization, including Lansky, Siegel, Vito Genovese, Frank Costello, Albert Anastasia, and Joe Adonis, felt that both of the Sicilian Mustache Petes were too obsessed with regional rivalries and outdated concepts

of honor to see the "big picture" with regard to the future of organized crime.

Luciano played a dangerous game. First he secretly went to Maranzano, offering to have Masseria killed in return for becoming Maranzano's second-in-command. On April 15, 1931, Luciano invited Masseria to a restaurant. Moments after Luciano excused himself to go to the restroom, four of his allies murdered Masseria. The Castellammarese War was over.

Maranzano soon grew uncomfortable with Luciano in his gang. He was afraid of the ambitious gangster and concerned because of his continued friendship with Jewish mobsters like Lansky and Siegel. Five months after the hit on Masseria, Maranzano asked Luciano to come to a meeting in his Manhattan office. However, Luciano was tipped off that Maranzano had hired the notorious Irish-American gunman Vincent "Mad Dog" Coll to assassinate him at the meeting. Luciano struck first. He sent five Jewish gunmen to Maranzano's office on September 10, 1931, where they killed the Mafia chief.

The elimination of Maranzano made Luciano the dominant crime boss in New York, and one of the most powerful in the country. One of his goals was to create a new system in which gangs could each control certain lucrative criminal activities in their territories and could settle disagreements without resorting to costly gang wars. On the advice of Johnny Torrio, Luciano created the Commission, a governing body for organized crime in the United States.

The Commission recognized five crime "families" in New York. In addition to Luciano's gang, the "five families" included the Gagliano (later Lucchese), Bonnano, Mangano (later Gambino), and Profaci (later Colombo) gangs. The Commission also included representatives of the Chicago Outfit and a crime family in Buffalo that controlled western New York state and Ohio. Later, crime families in Detroit, Los Angeles, Philadelphia, and other cities would be represented on the Commission.

Louis "Lepke" Buchalter

Luciano was the first chairman of the Commission.

The crime families were predominantly Italian, but Luciano continued to work with Jewish gangsters. Lansky and Siegel created a gang of enforcers that did the Commission's dirty work, making sure the crime families were feared. This group eventually became known in the press as "Murder Inc." because of the large number of contract killings it performed. In the 1930s and 1940s it was believed responsible for between 500 and 1,000 murders. The organization was later run by Jewish gangster Louis "Lepke" Buchalter and Albert "The Mad Hatter" Anastasia, an underboss of the Mangano crime family.

One of Murder Inc.'s most famous hits was the murder of New York gangster Dutch Schultz in 1935. Schultz was being hounded by a federal prosecutor,

Mobster Frank Costello was one of the most powerful members of the Luciano crime family. He would run the family on Lucky Luciano's behalf from 1937 until 1957, when he was forced out by Vito Genovese.

Thomas E. Dewey

Thomas Dewey, who was investigating organized crime in New York. Dewey had Schultz indicted twice on charges of tax evasion. Schultz beat the rap both times, but knew that Dewey would continue hounding him. He asked the Commission to authorize a hit on Dewey. Luciano and the Commission refused, because they knew that killing Dewey would bring even more federal attention to organized crime. Angry, Schultz said that he would kill Dewey anyway. Before he could do this, Luciano put out a contract on Schultz. On October 23, 1935, Murder Inc. hitmen Charles Workman and Emanuel "Mendy" Weiss killed Schultz and several of his bodyguards at a restaurant in Newark, New Jersey. After the murder, Luciano took over control of Schultz's lucrative gambling rackets.

Ironically, Luciano became the next high-profile target for the federal investigators led by Dewey. In 1936 Luciano was convicted of running illegal prostitution operations and sentenced to a minimum of 30 years in prison. He began his sentence at a remote prison in western New York. While Luciano was in prison he continued to run his crime family through his trusted underboss, Frank Costello.

Luciano's luck turned again during the early days of American involvement in World War II. U.S. leaders were afraid that German spies would try to sabotage warships in American ports. Government officials made a secret deal with Luciano. He promised to use his still-considerable influence with the mob to keep the docks safe. He also provided advice and useful Mafia contacts in Sicily before the 1943 Allied invasion of the island. In exchange, Luciano was transferred to a prison closer to New York City and given much better living conditions. The authorities also promised to release him from prison when the war ended.

The American troop transport USS *Lafayette* on fire in New York harbor, February 1942. Luciano's ally Albert Anastasia, who controlled the union dockworkers in New York, later claimed that he had engineered the fire on the *Lafayette* so that authorities would agree to free Luciano from prison, in exchange for mob "protection" of the harbor.

(Left) View of Havana, Cuba, in 1946, when Lucky Luciano held a Commission meeting in the city. The pretext for the meeting was the gangsters were visiting Cuba to see the famous Italian-American singer Frank Sinatra perform.

(Bottom) Lucky Luciano at a hotel in Rome in 1948, during his exile from the United States. The gangster continued to run his crime family, and also helped the Sicilian Mafia smuggle drugs to America.

By the time the war ended in 1945, Thomas Dewey was governor of New York. Dewey commuted Luciano's sentence, but insisted that he be deported back to Sicily. Luciano left the United States on February 10, 1946. He would never return.

The gangster was deeply upset by his exile from America, where he had lived most of his life. He soon secretly resettled in Cuba, only 90 miles away from Florida, so he could remain close to his criminal operations. While there, he met in December 1946 with the heads of the major crime families in Havana to discuss the future of organized crime.

When the the U.S. government learned Luciano was in Cuba, they insisted that Cuba deport him back to Sicily. He went back to the island in 1947 and spent his remaining days there, though he kept trying to return to the United States. Luciano continued to run his crime family through Costello until 1957, when Vito Genovese seized control and renamed the organization after himself.

Luciano died of a heart attack in 1962, while on on his way to the airport at Naples, Italy, to meet with a movie director who wanted to make a film about his life. (His conversations with the director would later be published as

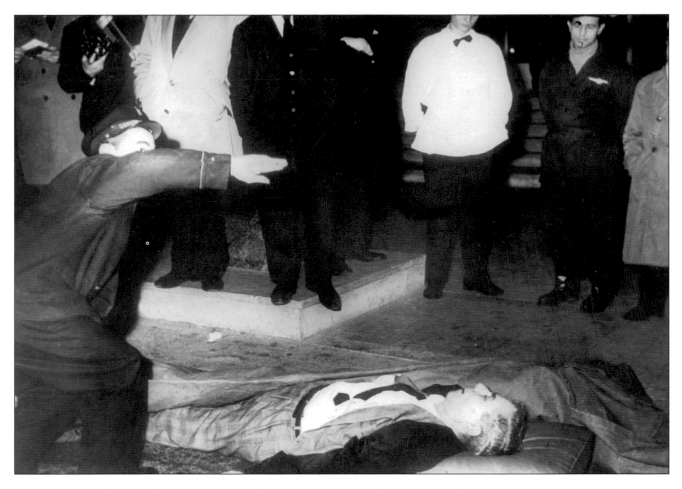

The body of Charles "Lucky" Luciano lies on the floor at the Naples Capodichino airport. Luciano died of a heart attack while at the airport on January 26, 1962.

a best-selling book, *The Last Testament of Lucky Luciano*, in 1974.) In death Luciano achieved something he couldn't in life—his body was returned to the United States, where it was buried in the family plot in St. John's Cemetery in Queens, New York.

Although Al Capone was the most famous mobster of the 1920s and 1930s, Charles Luciano was considerably more powerful and influential. As head of the Commission, he was able to control the actions of organized crime gangs throughout the country. The structure of crime families and the Commission that he created still exist today. Most experts agree that Luciano was one of the greatest criminal masterminds in American history.

An FBI agent once said of Meyer Lansky, "He would have been chairman of the board of General Motors if he'd gone into legitimate business." The Jewish-American mobster was a key figure in the development of organized crime, and during his lifetime earned hundreds of millions from his illegal activities.

MEYER LANSKY
GAMBLING KINGPIN

One of the most significant relationships in American organized crime began on a frigid afternoon in January of 1914. A scrawny 12-year-old Jewish boy named Meyer Lansky was hurrying to his home in New York City's Lower East Side. Suddenly a gang of Italian boys surrounded him, demanding protection money. At the time, Irish and Italian youth gangs preyed on anyone they caught alone. For a few pennies a week a Jewish boy like Lansky could purchase protection and escape beatings. On this day, the leader of the Italian gang was Salvatore Lucania. Lansky turned feisty and told Lucania—five years older and much bigger—that he was not going to pay. Lucania was so impressed with the boy's courage that he turned around and led his gang elsewhere.

Lansky had been born Maier Suchowljansky in the Russian Empire in 1902. At the time, Jews in the Russian Empire were often the focus of deadly attacks called pogroms. To escape the danger, the boy's father came to the United States in 1909. Two years later he brought over his family. He changed his son's name to Meyer Lansky to make it sound more American.

The Brooklyn neighborhood where Lansky lived teemed with craps games, and Lansky—an excellent student who did especially well in arithmetic—thought he could predict the odds and win. He was so confident that one day he gambled the family's money for *cholent*—a stew for the Sabbath midday meal. He lost. It was a painful, but useful, lesson.

Even when his father found him a job in a machine shop when he was 16, Lansky remained confident that he could become a successful gambler. There were plenty of games, and he was

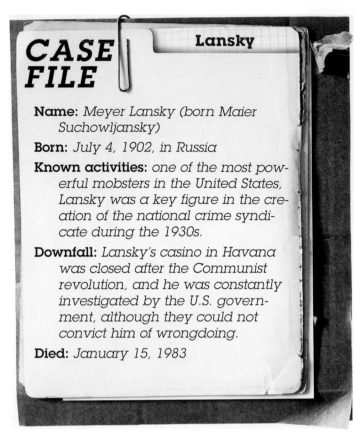

soon making much more money than he could in the machine shop.

As a teenager he also formed an alliance with Benjamin Siegel, another young Jew, as the heads of what became known as the Bugs and Meyer Gang. Whereas Lansky was highly intelligent and usually thought before acting, Siegel was the opposite. Even among gangsters he acquired a reputation for being particularly brutal. Siegel's nickname "Bugsy" wasn't a compliment; it referred to his tendency to go crazy, or "bugs," whenever he lost his temper—which happened frequently.

The Bugs and Meyer Gang became known for operating gambling games and running protection rackets on their Brooklyn turf. Gang members would go to other parts of Manhattan to commit robberies and burglaries or to steal cars. Other members of the gang included Abner "Longie" Zwillman, Louis "Lepke" Buchalter, and Dutch Schultz. All would go on to infamous careers in organized crime.

Another chance meeting, this one in 1920, changed the course of Meyer Lansky's life. While attending a bar mitzvah for the son of a friend, he met Arnold Rothstein, the semi-legendary ruler of the New York underworld. The teenager must have been in awe when Rothstein began talking with him and invited him to dinner. Rothstein had an agenda: he wanted to recruit Lansky and his gang to work for him.

Rothstein recognized the immense profits that could be made by providing illegal liquor to satisfy the national thirst for alcohol that Prohibition created. He needed men to help with the actual mechanics of the bootlegging operation, but felt that more established gangs, such as the Sicilian Mafia, weren't suitable. The "Mustache Petes" were too set in their ways and were unwilling to work with non-Italians. Lansky's gang—made up of both Jewish and Italian youths—was much more flexible. And because they were young, Rothstein felt he could mold them.

"We sat talking for six hours," Lansky said much later. "It was a big surprise to me. Rothstein told me quite frankly that he picked me because I was ambitious and 'hungry.' But I felt I had nothing to lose. He knew I was working with Charles Lucania—as he was still known—and that we could call upon our friends, the mixture of Jews and Italians who were loyal to us."

The arrangement proved incredibly beneficial for both sides, especially since Rothstein proved to be an ideal mentor for his young colleagues as they assembled the largest liquor-smuggling operation in the country. By this point Lucania had adopted the name Charles Luciano, in part because he thought it was easier for his Jewish friends to pronounce. Eventually he acquired the nickname of "Lucky."

Lansky realized that Prohibition wouldn't last forever. In the early 1930s, almost without missing a beat, he began to shift his focus back to gambling. He opened a casino in Saratoga Springs, New York. Soon he had a string of "carpet joints," as gambling houses that featured honest games were known. Patrons thronged to these casinos because the games were fair. They didn't need to be rigged. Lansky's casinos were highly profitable because of his ability to calculate the odds in his favor. Lansky opened additional carpet joints in Florida, New Orleans, and Cuba.

At the same time, Luciano and Lansky began putting a national crime syndicate into place. As historian Carl Sifakis notes, "They were the perfect match: the well-read, even studious Lansky, who could survey all the angles of a given situation, and the less-than-erudite Luciano . . . who made up for his limitations with a brilliant flair for organization and the brutal character to set any plan in motion."

Not even Luciano's imprisonment in 1936 could prevent the national crime syndicate from controlling criminal activities in the United States. The syndicate expanded westward, with Lansky sending Siegel to California in the late 1930s to organize rackets in the West. Siegel's good looks and dangerous charm helped him become a celebrity among the movie stars of Los Angeles.

In 1946, Siegel took over the construction of a hotel and casino in the small town of Las Vegas, Nevada, one of the few places in the country where gambling was legal. Lansky and other crime lords backed him financially.

Benjamin "Bugsy" Siegel

However, the Flamingo Hotel, which opened in December 1946, was not financially successful and the mobsters lost most of their investment. Siegel was blamed for the failure and was executed in 1947. Lansky had tried to protect his friend as long as possible, but most people believe that he ultimately signed off on the hit.

Nevada was not the only spot where the mob wanted to promote gambling during the late 1940s. Lansky made a profitable agreement with Cuban president Fulgencio Batista, who allowed the syndicate to run casinos and horse racing tracks on the island. Luciano had been deported from the United States to Sicily after his release from prison, but he secretly came to Havana so he could continue to run the criminal organization in America.

The law finally caught up with Meyer Lansky in 1953. He was indicted in New York on numerous counts of illegal betting. He pleaded guilty to some of the charges and spent three months in prison. This was the only time that Lansky would see the inside of a cell.

After being released from prison, Lansky returned to Cuba. Batista gave Lansky the authority to make sure that Cuba's casinos were run fairly. This soon became a very profitable project for both men. Lansky even built his own casino. However, in 1959 Fidel Castro organized a successful Communist revolution that overthrew Batista's government. When the Communists came to

The Flamingo Hotel and Casino as it appeared in 1947, when Lansky's longtime friend Bugsy Siegel was killed, probably on Lansky's orders, for mismanaging the mob-funded project.

power, they destroyed the casinos and threw out the mobsters. This was a severe financial blow to Lansky, who fled Cuba and moved to Florida.

Although during the 1960s and 1970s Meyer Lansky was not permitted to own casinos in Las Vegas because of his connections to organized crime. Despite this, Lansky had substantial interests in some of Vegas's most successful hotels. His share of the profits enabled him to live comfortably. Yet as author Richard Russo notes, "Lansky was smart. He didn't live lavishly, like Al Capone. He knew that every line of his tax return was going to be scrutinized."

The U.S. Department of Justice put out a considerable effort to investigate Lansky. It even formed a special task force in the late 1960s to try to find incriminating evidence against him. According to wiretaps, Lansky once boasted that organized crime was far larger than U.S. Steel, one of the biggest American corporations.

Faced with the likelihood of being charged with income tax evasion, in 1970 Lansky fled to Israel. That country had a law allowing any Jew to move there. However, his arrival led to a legal battle in the country that lasted for more than two years. Finally the courts decided that he posed a danger to Israeli society and ordered him to leave. In 1972, when Lansky returned to the United States, he was indicted for mul-

Meyer Lansky in 1958, the year his casino in Cuba, the Hotel Habana Riviera, earned the gangster a profit of more than $3 million. However, Lansky was forced to flee the country in early 1959 when the Batista government was overthrown by Communists.

tiple crimes. However, the evidence against him was weak and Lansky was acquitted in 1974.

After this, Meyer Lansky lived quietly in Miami Beach, dying of cancer early in 1983.

THE PURPLE GANG
FEARED BOOTLEGGERS

There are several theories about how the Purple Gang, a violent criminal organization that cut a brief but bloody path through Detroit at the height of the Prohibition era, got its name. One is that an early victim told police, "They're tainted, those boys. Their characters are off-color. They're purple. They'll come to a bad end." Another theory is that one of the group's early members was a hood named Sammy "Purple" Cohen. A third theory about the name is that it refers to the process of dying, or coloring, garments, because the Purple Gang was heavily involved with the union that did such work in the Detroit area.

And while the gang members themselves almost certainly didn't make the association, purple happens to be the color most closely associated with royalty. This is appropriate since during the 1920s the Purple Gang ruled the Detroit underworld. The organization has been accused of committing as many as 500 murders—a considerably higher body count than even Chicago, which was notorious for its gangland slayings.

The Purple Gang was a Jewish street gang. Many of its members had been born in eastern Europe and had come to America around the end of the 19th century. The group's leaders were four brothers—Raymond, Joseph, Abe, and Isadore "Izzy" Bernstein—who had immigrated from Russia to New York, then moved to Detroit.

The Bernstein family was very poor, and the brothers became petty criminals who enlisted school friends in their activities, according to a report in the *Detroit Free Press*. "The boys snatched ice cream, gum, candy, cookies and fruit from hucksters and stores," the *Press* reported. "They ganged up on children their own age, sometimes they strong-armed grownups."

In 1920, when Prohibition went into effect, Detroit was riding a huge boom in population due to the rapid growth of the American auto industry. It had become the nation's fourth-largest city, with a population of nearly a million people. Detroit is located on the border with Canada, which in the 1920s permitted the distillation of alcohol for sale to other countries. Rum-runners who could smuggle Canadian whiskey and beer into the United States were sure to make a fortune.

The Detroit River, which forms the border with Canada, was a smuggler's paradise. In places it is less than half a mile wide and contains numerous small coves, which enabled anyone with a small boat to join in the lucrative rum-running trade. Things got even easier for bootleggers during the winter, when the river froze over and the hours of darkness increased. Trucks packed with Canadian booze could speed across the ice to the United States. During Prohibition, it is estimated that 75 percent of the illegal liquor smuggled into the United States passed through the Detroit area.

At the start of Prohibition, the Purple Gang became involved in more serious, and lucrative, crimes. They started working for Charles Leiter and Henry Shorr, a pair of older mobsters who helped the gang with a variety of illicit activities, including armed robberies and extortion rackets. They were particularly feared as hijackers. As historian Paul Kavieff explains:

> They were a predatory group and they were known for their ruthlessness, I mean they shot everybody during these hijackings, even the guys who were simply driving the trucks. What that resulted in was that if you were making a beer delivery and were robbed by the Purples, you fought to the death, because you knew that the Purples were going to haul you out of the truck and kill you anyway.

The Purple Gang would turn the hijacked alcohol over to Leiter and Shorr, or they would sell it themselves. They had no problem finding customers. By 1925, there were about 25,000 speakeasies operating in Detroit. The Bernstein brothers invested some of their profits in bribing the police and civic officials to turn a blind eye to their activity. They also took control of Detroit's illegal gambling, prostitution, and drug trade, and became heavily involved in labor unions.

In the mid-1920s, gang members formed the Wholesale Cleaners and Dyers Association. This union promised to set prices and stabilize the market for clothing cleaners and dyers. In reality the Purples were running a protection racket. The Purple Gang would "persuade" anyone who wasn't a member to join, which involved paying dues to the organization. Businesses that refused were vandalized, and sometimes destroyed by fire or bombings. Several cleaners who refused to pay the gang were murdered. Over the next three years the Purple Gang waged the "Cleaners and Dyers War," using the dues money they extorted to fund their illegal activities.

The Purple Gang made most of its money from bootlegging, and throughout the mid-1920s fought regularly with Irish and Italian gangs for control of territory. The gang often used violence as a way to warn rivals not to try cutting in on their business. In 1927, for example, when a liquor distributor associated with the gang was killed, the Purple Gang invited the three gunmen they suspected of the murder to a "peace conference" at the Miraflores Apartments in Detroit. The three men were members of a gang from St. Louis who wanted to set up shop in Detroit. The Purple Gang let their own guns—including a Thompson machine gun, the first time the infamous "Tommy gun" was used in a gang-related crime in Detroit—do the talking. The three St. Louis mobsters were so riddled with bullets they could barely be recognized.

The Purple Gang was so feared they could tell even Al Capone to back off. Because of Detroit's easy access to Canadian liquor and its tens of thousands of auto workers who had money

to spend on alcohol thanks to the boom in auto production, Capone wanted to expand his operation into Detroit. However, when he visited the city in 1927 the Purple Gang threatened him with an all-out war. Capone compromised, agreeing to limit him activities to the western half of Michigan, which was directly across Lake Michigan from his base in Chicago. He also agreed to purchase Canadian liquor from the Purple Gang.

This arrangement worked well for both sides. There is considerable evidence that the Purple Gang helped Capone carry out the St. Valentine's Day Massacre in February 1929. The gang arranged for a shipment of alcohol to be delivered to Capone's rival, George "Bugs" Moran. It was a setup. Posing as police officers, several mob gunmen—probably including at least two members of the Purple Gang—slaughtered seven members of Moran's North Side Gang while they waited for the shipment to arrive. Moran was the intended target, but fortunately for him he did not show up at the warehouse where the massacre occurred.

The so-called Cleaners and Dyers War ended in 1928, when Abe Bernstein, Ray Bernstein, and 11 other gang members were placed on trial for extortion. However, Detroit cleaners were so afraid of the Purple Gang that they refused to testify against them. In

The Detroit skyline as seen from Windsor, Canada, in the late 1920s—a time when the city was ruled by the Purple Gang. Detroit was a critical city for bootleggers because they could easily smuggle high-quality Canadian alcohol across the Detroit River border with the United States.

addition, critical evidence "disappeared" before the trial began. In September 1928, all of the gang members were acquitted.

At this point, the Purple Gang was at the height of its power. Its control over the Detroit rackets was unquestioned, and the gang's leaders had grown wealthy. They ate in the city's best restaurants, lived in elegant houses, and wore expensive clothing. Abe Bernstein became friends with New York mobsters like Meyer Lansky and Joe Adonis, with whom he owned several casinos in Miami. However, the gang's days at the top were numbered.

In the fall of 1931, the American Legion planned to hold a national convention in Detroit. Gangs knew there would be a huge demand for liquor, and this resulted in a rash of hijackings. To help protect their liquor shipments, the Purple Gang imported three gunmen from Chicago, Joseph Lebowitz,

Detroit police inspect equipment found in an underground brewery, early 1930s. The end of Prohibition eliminated the Purple Gang's largest source of revenue. Within a few years, the Italian-American crime family of Joseph Zerelli had eliminated the once-feared Jewish gang, taking control of the rackets in Detroit.

Herman Paul, and Isadore "the Rat" Sutker. The trio soon decided to break away and start their own organization, the Third Avenue Terrors.

Ray Bernstein developed a plan that would eliminate this threat to the Purple Gang's control of Detroit. He reached out to the Terrors through a mutual associate, a bookmaker named Solly Levine, asking him to arrange a meeting on September 16, 1931, at an apartment on Collingwood Avenue.

Levine brought the three men to the apartment where, after a few minutes of conversation, Ray Bernstein left the room saying he needed to call the accountant who kept the gang's financial records. He had actually gone outside to start a getaway car. When they heard the car engine start, three other members of the Purple Gang opened fire, killing the three hoods. They grabbed the shaken Levine and ran outside to Bernstein and the getaway car.

The "Collingwood Manor Massacre" created a sensation. Letting Levine live turned out to be a mistake. Bernstein had apparently intended to frame Levine for the murders, but the bookmaker was arrested before he could do so. Although at first Levine denied knowing anything about the crime, he soon broke down and told police who had done the shooting.

Not even the large sums of money the Purple Gang had used to bribe police and local politicians could help them this time. The Collingwood slayings had resulted in intense publicity and generated civic outrage. Within a few days, Bernstein and two of the three shooters were arrested, their hiding places revealed by anonymous tips from members of rival gangs who wanted to see the Purple Gang weakened. In November 1931, thanks to Levine's tes-timony, Bernstein and the others were convicted and sentenced to life in prison without parole. (Soon after the trial, Levine disappeared. No one knows whether he started another life under a new identity, or became a victim of gang retribution.)

The convictions, along with the growing power of Italian-American crime families under Lucky Luciano's National Crime Syndicate, broke the Purple Gang. Some of the gang's members moved west, setting up operations in California. The repeal of Prohibition in 1933 took away the gang's primary source of revenue. Joe and Izzy Bernstein ran a wire service that provided horse-racing results to gambling houses. Abe Bernstein operated his Miami casinos and tried to get his brother Ray freed from prison. He also served as an advisor to other mobsters, including Joseph Zerelli, whose Sicilian mafia organization had taken control of Detroit's rackets by the late 1930s.

It is often reported that, with Abe Bernstein's blessing, Zerelli's men killed the Purple Gang's last active member, Harry Millman, in November, 1937. By then Zerelli was firmly established as Detroit's crime boss, a position he maintained until his death in 1977.

Mickey Cohen stands among the front pages of newspapers that helped make him the most infamous resident of Los Angeles in the 1950s. Like his idol Al Capone, Cohen enjoyed being the center of media attention. At the same time he was running criminal rackets in California and Nevada, Cohen socialized publicly with movie stars, politicians, and members of Western high society.

MICKEY COHEN
HOLLYWOOD GANGSTER

Many gang leaders prefer to remain anonymous and away from the harsh spotlight of public life. Not Mickey Cohen. Like Al Capone, his idol and in some ways his role model, Cohen could be charming and charismatic and loved being in the limelight. As Tere Tereba, who wrote a biography about Cohen, once explained:

> A self-creation, Mickey Cohen made himself into a real life "Hollywood" gangster—deadly, brazen, and florid. He got more ink than major stars. . . . Everyone knew he was dangerous. He was the mob boss of L.A —and hardly tried to hide it. He lived his life in Technicolor and wide screen.

Born in Brooklyn, New York, on September 4, 1913, Cohen moved with his mother to Los Angeles soon afterward when his father died. With his mother working to support six children, the boy had little supervision. He became involved in crime by the time he was eight, helping his older brother Harry deliver bootleg alcohol. Harry also took young Mickey along when he went gambling at night, telling his little brother to sleep in the car when he got tired. Though Mickey's schooling suffered, he acquired "street smarts."

Another element of Mickey Cohen's education involved learning how to box. By the time he was 11, he was fighting regularly in amateur bouts, and entertaining thoughts of becoming a professional boxer. He also became a street hustler, slowly amassing a significant amount of cash and nurturing a lifelong love of money.

When Mickey Cohen's mother remarried, he moved to Cleveland to be with his brother Harry. He continued to be involved in the boxing scene, and eventually began to fight professionally. Mobsters were heavily involved in box-

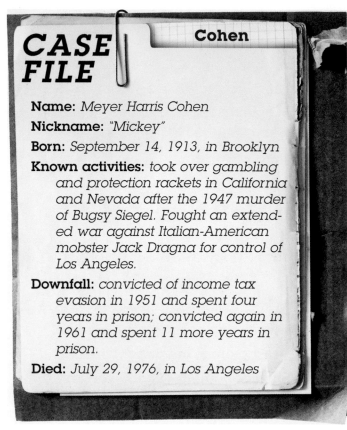

CASE FILE

Cohen

Name: *Meyer Harris Cohen*

Nickname: *"Mickey"*

Born: *September 14, 1913, in Brooklyn*

Known activities: *took over gambling and protection rackets in California and Nevada after the 1947 murder of Bugsy Siegel. Fought an extended war against Italian-American mobster Jack Dragna for control of Los Angeles.*

Downfall: *convicted of income tax evasion in 1951 and spent four years in prison; convicted again in 1961 and spent 11 more years in prison.*

Died: *July 29, 1976, in Los Angeles*

ing at the time, and Cohen took notice of how well the top figures in organized crime lived. Cohen sometimes worked as an enforcer for Cleveland gangsters and bootleggers named Lou Rothkopf and Moe Dalitz. He later moved to New York to further his boxing career, and also worked for other mobsters. Finally, Cohen moved to Chicago, where he ran a gambling operation for Al Capone's outfit, and later worked for Capone's successor, Jake "Greasy Thumb" Guzik. Although he was small, standing only 5 feet 5 inches as an adult, he was feared and respected for his toughness.

The height of Cohen's boxing career occurred in June 1931, when he got a title shot against the World Feather-

weight Champion, Tommy Paul. Cohen was knocked out in the first round. After this, Cohen continued fighting for a couple of years but spent more time involved in organized crime activities. A dispute with another Chicago gangster forced him to leave the city, so he returned to Cleveland.

In 1937 his mentor Rothkopf sent Cohen to Los Angeles, where he was assigned as a bodyguard to Benjamin "Bugsy" Siegel, one of the mob's top hit men. Meyer Lansky and Lucky Luciano wanted Siegel to establish a profitable new criminal organization on the West Coast on behalf of the established New York crime families, despite the fact that Los Angeles already had a criminal organization headed by Jack Dragna. The New York families were wealthier and more powerful, so Dragna had little choice but to let Siegel operate. The two mobsters formed an uneasy alliance that turned out to be highly profitable for both gangs.

Cohen found living in California to his liking. A Jewish American, Cohen was aware of the restrictions that Nazi dictator Adolf Hitler had placed on German Jews during the late 1930s. One time he was briefly locked up in the Los Angeles County jail. When two American Nazis were placed in the same cell, Cohen beat them up. Word got out, and Cohen was occasionally called upon to break up Nazi rallies.

"Nobody could pay me for this work," he later said. "It was my patriotic duty. There ain't no amount of money to buy them kind of things."

Cohen's patriotism only went so far, however. He got married just a few hours before registering for the military draft in 1940, because at the time married men were exempt from being drafted. In his registration, he also emphasized his many criminal experiences, knowing that this would lead him to be declared unfit for service in the military.

Despite his effort to avoid military service during the Second World War (1939-1945), Cohen still saw plenty of action. Siegel's organization was involved in labor strikes and extorted money from movie studios and famous actors. Those who tried to resist were beaten or murdered.

In 1945 a Los Angeles nightclub owner named William Wilkerson decided to build a luxury hotel and casino in Nevada, one of the few places in the United States where gambling was legal. He chose Las Vegas, which at the time was a small town in the desert with a population of around 10,000. Wilkerson planned to create a resort that would attract celebrity high rollers from Hollywood and Los Angeles. He needed funding for the project, which he received from Bugsy Siegel. However, Siegel soon forced Wilkerson out and took over control of the hotel,

which was called the Flamingo.

The move turned out to be a mistake. Siegel did not manage the hotel construction properly, and it cost millions more than expected. The casino opened in December 1946, but was not immediately profitable. With their losses mounting, New York gang leaders ordered Siegel to be killed in August 1947.

This turned out to be a great opportunity for Mickey Cohen. "I took over from Benny [Siegel] right away on instructions from the people back east," Cohen later said. "Naturally, I missed Benny, but to be honest with you, his getting knocked off was not a bad break for me. Pretty soon I was running everything out here."

With Bugsy Siegel gone, Dragna quickly acted to remove his new rival for control of West Coast crime. Dragna's organization made several attempts on Cohen's life. One time, a car pulled alongside Cohen while he was driving in Los Angeles. Shotgun blasts blew out the windows. Cohen laid across the driver's seat on his side and still managed to steer the car. Another time, he was leaving a restaurant and happened to bend over as bullets zipped through the space where his head had been. In February 1950 Dragna's men set off dynamite at Cohen's house while he and his wife were sleeping. The house was badly damaged but they were

Mickey Cohen survived 11 attempts on his life during the years he ruled organized crime in Los Angeles.

not harmed. Reporters noted that after the bombing, Cohen seemed more distressed at losing 40 expensive suits than the attempt on his life.

Although Meyer Lansky had advised Cohen to keep a low profile, the gangster couldn't resist associating with Los Angeles civic leaders and entertainment industry figures. Soon Cohen had become something of a celebrity himself. In 1950 *Life* magazine, one of the nation's most popular publications, even ran a photo spread about him, entitled

"The Quiet Home Life of a Shy Businessman." In the accompanying article, Cohen said that he was being unfairly harassed by the Los Angeles Police Department and told *Life*, "I take my oath on my mother, my wife, and my dogs—and I'm very fond of my dogs—I ain't guilty of what they say about me."

Neither Dragna nor the LAPD could catch up with Cohen, but federal authorities were more successful. In November 1950 he was ordered to testify before the U.S. Senate's Select Committee to Investigate Crime in Interstate Commerce (better known as the Kefauver Committee). During the hearing, New Hampshire Senator Charles Tobey repeatedly called Cohen a hoodlum and asked, "Is it not a fact that you live extravagantly, surrounded by violence?" Cohen replied, "Whaddya mean 'surrounded by violence?' People are shooting at *me!*" Members of the committee did not have much sympathy for Cohen, who vehemently denied any wrongdoing.

However, Cohen had made a serious error in judgment. Most mobsters were careful to hide their considerable earnings behind shell companies or by buying into legitimate businesses. Cohen didn't. "Mickey maintained that he was just a former bookmaker who now earned a modest living from gambling," writes mob historian John Buntin. "But he lived like a pasha in a $120,000 house in Brentwood and purchased new Cadillacs every year for himself and his wife (to say nothing of his $15,000 armored car). Anyone who bothered to do a quick back-of-the-envelope calculation could see that there was something suspicious about such lavish expenditures." As a result of the Kefauver Committee's investigation, Cohen was convicted of income tax evasion in 1951. He spent four years in prison.

When Cohen got out, he resumed his lavish public lifestyle. If anything, he became even more famous. He was not afraid to speak to reporters, even talking about his involvement in organized crime—something that angered many of his mob associates. During one interview with television personality Mike Wallace, he said, "I have killed no man that in the first place didn't deserve killing by the standards of our way of life."

Mickey Cohen wasn't through with organized crime, and the government wasn't through with him. A three-year investigation of his finances turned up plenty of evidence that Cohen was once again hiding illegally gotten money. In 1961 he was convicted of income tax evasion again, and was sent to Alcatraz to serve his sentence. While there, Cohen was badly injured by an inmate who beat him with an iron pipe. Partially paralyzed and suffering from stomach cancer, Mickey Cohen was released from prison in 1972. He died four years later.

After Mickey Cohen's 1951 conviction, his rival Jack Dragna took over most of his rackets in Los Angeles. When Dragna died in 1956, members of the Chicago Outfit became heavily involved in the Los Angeles rackets. Las Vegas became an "open" city where any mob family could work. Today the Italian crime family in Los Angeles is one of the weaker mafia families. It struggles for control of the city with the many street gangs in Los Angeles, such as the Bloods, the Crips, the Hells Angels, Mara Salvatrucha, and the Rascals.

The highest-profile mobster of the 1980s and 1990s was John Gotti, who became a favorite of the media because of his style and outgoing personality. Arrested and charged with crimes on several occasions between 1986 and 1991, Gotti managed to avoid being convicted. This led to his nickname as the "Teflon Don," because criminal charges would not stick to him.

JOHN GOTTI
THE TEFLON DON

The film industry has always been fascinated with mobsters and often creates memorable gangland characters. For example, the 1932 movie *Scarface* capitalized on the notoriety of Al Capone. Fascination with the mafia peaked after the release of *The Godfather* in 1972. Starring Marlon Brando as Don Vito Corleone, the film created a sensation and is widely regarded as one of the greatest movies ever made. Two sequels followed, in 1974 and 1990. Writer Peter Maas notes that the *Godfather* movies:

> took an intricately structured "other" world . . . populated with people you could root for or against. . . . The *Godfather* saga contained everything that concerned and excited us: family, romance, betrayal, power, lust, greed, legitimacy, even salvation. And all played out on a grand stage, with death, inevitable and often violent, waiting in the wings."

For those interested in the mob, the *Godfather* films filled a void in the 1970s and 1980s. In the past, gangsters like Capone and Mickey Cohen had high profiles, and their exploits often made the front pages of newspapers. They even posed for eager photographers. But once the government began to crack down on organized crime during the 1960s, mob leaders began to keep a much lower profile. They preferred to conduct their business as far from public scrutiny as possible. Mob bosses preferred to avoid widespread media attention—at least until a charismatic gangster named John Gotti emerged as a public figure during the mid-1980s.

During the last two decades of the 20th century, John Gotti was the world's most infamous mobster. "Gotti thoroughly dominated his era, orchestrating dozens of murders—and making it

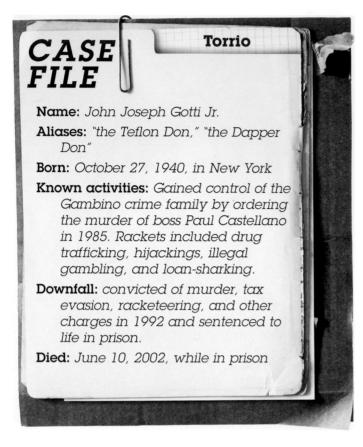

CASE FILE

Torrio

Name: *John Joseph Gotti Jr.*

Aliases: *"the Teflon Don," "the Dapper Don"*

Born: *October 27, 1940, in New York*

Known activities: *Gained control of the Gambino crime family by ordering the murder of boss Paul Castellano in 1985. Rackets included drug trafficking, hijackings, illegal gambling, and loan-sharking.*

Downfall: *convicted of murder, tax evasion, racketeering, and other charges in 1992 and sentenced to life in prison.*

Died: *June 10, 2002, while in prison*

impossible, because of his fame and flamboyance and pure viciousness, for anyone to be a mobster in quite that way again," writes crime author Steve Fishman. " 'You'll never see another one like me,' he once said."

Gotti seemed an unlikely candidate for stardom. Born in 1940, he was one of 13 children and grew up in poverty. When he was 16, he was struck by a cement truck. It crushed his leg and four toes, leaving him with a permanent limp. He had to drop out of school—something he later admitted that he regretted. Soon afterward, he met Carmine Fatico, a caporegime of the Gambino crime family.

The family had been named for

Carlo Gambino, a small, retiring man who hardly seemed like a mob boss. A fellow gangster once derisively referred to Gambino as a "squirrel of a man, a servile and cringing individual." But like another small man—Meyer Lansky, under whom he had gotten his start during the 1930s—Gambino had a shrewd intelligence. He used that intelligence to rise to the leadership of what had once been Lucky Luciano's criminal organization in New York, giving the family his own name in 1957.

The Gambino family was generally considered to be the most powerful and wealthiest of New York's so-called "Five Families." By the 1960s, when John Gotti began working as one of several hundred members of Fatico's crew, the Gambino family was earning $500 million a year from illegal activities, including gambling, prostitution, extortion, and the hijacking of valuable cargos that were sold on the black market.

Gotti began his criminal career under Fatico's guidance by committing a series of hijackings. He was arrested and imprisoned from 1969 to 1972. After being released on parole, Gotti made a name for himself as a Gambino enforcer. In 1973 he helped in the killing of James McBratney, an Irish-American gangster who had kidnapped and murdered Gambino's nephew.

Gotti was a rising star in the Gambino family. When Fatico himself was sent to prison in 1976, Gotti was officially inducted into the family (becoming a "made man") and was named caporegime in charge of Fatico's crew. He reported to family underboss Aniello Dellacroce.

The family itself was going through a major period of change. Carlo Gambino had appointed his brother-in-law Paul Castellano, the family's other underboss, to take over the family when he died of a heart attack in 1976. Many of Dellacroce's men did not like Castellano and believed Dellacroce should have been named head of the family. Dellacroce ordered his men to respect Gambino's wishes, but the succession resulted in tension within the family.

Despite this snub to Dellacroce, a man he greatly respected, Gotti continued to make money for the crime family. In his personal life,

however, the mobster suffered a major loss in 1980, when a neighbor accidentally killed his youngest son, Frank, in a minibike accident. Not long afterward, the neighbor disappeared. Gotti was vacationing in Florida at the time, and no evidence ever linked him to the disappearance. However, many people believe he ordered the unfortunate man to be executed.

By the mid-1980s, Gotti had grown dissatisfied with the way Castellano was

John Gotti (center) speaks to his childhood friend and fellow made man Angelo Ruggiero (left). With them is Gambino family caporegime Carmine Fatico, Gotti's mentor in the mob. This surveillance photo was taken in front of the Bergin Hunt and Fish Club in Queens, New York, where Fatico's crew made its headquarters.

DAILY ⊙ NEWS

35¢   NEW YORK'S PICTURE NEWSPAPER®   Tuesday, December 17, 1985

RUBOUT

MOB HITS BIG PAUL
Body of Thomas Bilotti lies by his car on E. 46th St. after Bilotti and Paul (Big Paul) Castellano, 70, were shot to death by three men who fled last night. At the time of his death, Big Paul was reputedly the boss of the nation's biggest crime family. **Stories start on page 2; other pictures in centerfold.**

The *New York Daily News* reports on the murder of Gambino crime family head Paul Castellano, which was orchestrated by John Gotti.

If appearances were everything, John Gotti would have been one of the most successful mob bosses in history. He took great care to appear immaculately groomed every time he went out in public. He wore expensive suits, handmade silk ties, and flashy jewelry. He threw lavish parties and ate at New York's finest restaurants.

Unlike other mafia leaders, Gotti loved to be in the public eye. He was happy to pose for photos and speak to reporters, and was always ready with a quip. Perhaps his most famous came when a reporter asked him if he was the head of the Gambino Family. "Sure, I'm the boss of the family—my wife and kids," he jokingly responded. The media, in turn, was thrilled with the appearance of a gangster who appeared to be a real-life Godfather. They quickly dubbed him the "Dapper Don."

But the reality was very different. "*The Godfather* gave Gotti a romantic view of his own brutal life," notes Nicholas Pileggi, who has written many books on organized crime in America. "Those films gave Gotti a sense of dignity and history. They changed the way gangsters thought of themselves. In their heads, they became Brando and De Niro. But the problem is that Gotti was just a high-school dropout and a degenerate gambler."

running the family. It was clear that Castellano didn't think much of Gotti, either. Dellacroce tried to keep peace in the Gambino family, but after his death from cancer in early December 1985, Gotti believed that Castellano would try to have him killed. He decided to strike first. On December 16, 1985, he watched from a nearby car as some of his men shot Castellano to death outside Sparks Steak House in Manhattan. Soon after this, Gotti was named head of the Gambino family.

At first Gotti's background didn't seem to matter. On three occasions in the 1980s authorities indicted him for criminal activities. All three times Gotti was acquitted, leading to another nickname—the "Teflon Don," because the government's criminal charges would not stick to him.

But the government never gave up. Gotti's desire for publicity made it easy to track his movements. They knew where he held high-level meetings with his underlings, and managed to install bugs that enabled them to listen in on his conversations. In some of those conversations, Gotti discussed the murder of Castellano as well as other hits. In one chilling sequence, federal authorities recorded Gotti explaining why he had ordered the 1990 murder of another Gambino family member, Louie DiBono: "You know why he's dying? He's gonna die because he refused to come in when I called. He didn't do nothing else wrong."

In December 1990 the FBI and New York police arrested Gotti and two other top members of the Gambino family, underboss Sammy "The Bull" Gravano and consigliere Frank "Frankie Loc" LoCascio. Using their recorded conversations, the government indicted Gotti on more than 40 charges that included murder, loan sharking, and racketeering.

To be certain that they could convict the Teflon Don, federal prosecutors made a deal with Gravano, one of Gotti's closest associates. Gravano had been involved in the 1985 murder of Castellano, and Gotti had made him underboss of his former crew when he became head of the Gambino family. In fact, Gotti expected that if he was sent to prison Gravano would run the family's operations on his behalf. However,

Testimony from Gotti associate Salvatore "Sammy the Bull" Gravano helped federal prosecutors convict the Teflon Don in 1992.

Mugshots taken after Gotti's arrest on December 11, 1990.

the FBI had recorded conversations in which Gotti disparaged Gravano, which they played for the underboss when he was arrested. Angry at being insulted, and hoping to avoid prison, Gravano agreed to testify against Gotti and LoCascio at trial.

That testimony sealed Gotti's fate. The jury only deliberated 14 hours before finding Gotti guilty of all the charges on April 2, 1992. A jubilant James Fox, director of the FBI's New York office, announced at a press conference, "The Teflon is gone. The don is covered with Velcro, and all the charges stuck."

Not everyone was happy about the verdict. In June 1992, when Gotti was sentenced to life imprisonment without possibility of parole, a crowd of more than 1,000 people chanting "Free John Gotti" and "Freedom for John" tried to storm the courthouse. More than 100

additional New York policemen rushed to the scene to reinforce the badly outnumbered guards. Some were attacked so viciously that they needed medical attention.

The nearly mythic admiration that Gotti inspired resulted in hundreds of fan letters to him during the early years of his confinement. Some letters even asked for his advice on dealing with personal problems. One said, "I am writing to see if you would write a letter of encouragement to my aunt who is terminally ill with cancer. She and I both are great admirers of yours and if anyone knows about courage it's you." Gotti, aware that a personal letter could become a valuable collector's item from which he would derive no benefit, had his lawyer respond to the woman and tell her to remain strong.

For Gotti himself, "remaining strong" became increasingly difficult. He was locked in virtual isolation in a cell measuring eight feet by seven feet, spending all but one hour a day there. In 1998 he developed throat cancer. Though the tumor was removed, the cancer returned two years later and Gotti's condition rapidly worsened. In the past many gangsters, including Al Capone, had been released from prison on humanitarian grounds when it was evident that they had serious, life-threatening illnesses. Not Gotti. Many people believe that the federal govern-

The body of former mob boss John Gotti is carried from Papavero Funeral Home in Queens, June 15, 2002. Gotti is buried in St John's cemetery in New York. Not far away are the graves of several other infamous New York mobsters, Charles "Lucky" Luciano and Carlo Gambino.

ment wanted to make an example of him. He died in prison in June 2002.

Before John Gotti died, four films had already been made about his life. His death was hardly the end of the media fascination with the Teflon Don. His son John Gotti Jr. was acting head of the Gambino family from 1992 until his own arrest in 1999. After his release in 2005, he was tried four times on racketeering charges. All four ended in mistrials. After the last one the government announced it wouldn't seek any more trials. The media immediately referred to him as "Teflon Jr." Gotti's daughter Victoria became a newspaper columnist, book author, and star of a short-lived TV reality series called *Growing up Gotti*. And a new film, *Gotti: Three Generations*, starring John Travolta as the gangster, is scheduled to be released in 2014.

BRIGHTON BEACH BUSINESS IMPROVEMENT DISTRICT · B.K.

BRIGHTON BEACH

AVENUE

Welcome
to
Brighton Beach

Little Russia
by the Sea

BRIGHTON BEACH BID

Brighton Beach in Brooklyn is considered a center of Russian mafiya activity in the United States.

THE RUSSIAN MAFIYA
A NEW CRIMINAL EMPIRE

The Russian mafia, or mafiya as it is also known, consists of thousands of crime syndicates, most of which originated during the era of the Soviet Union (1917–1991). Some of those syndicates expanded their operations internationally after 1991, when the Soviet Union disintegrated.

Many of today's Russian mafiya groups originated in the Soviet system of prison camps known as *gulags*, which operated from the late 1920s until the mid-1950s. Within the gulags, criminal gangs formed that eventually gained control over many activities. Once the gulags were closed, many criminals were released back into Soviet society. Leaders of the gulag gangs were determined to do whatever it took to thrive, and often formed partnerships with corrupt political leaders.

In the Communist system, the government controlled the factories and businesses. It was supposed to provide food, consumer goods, and other things that the Soviet people would need to survive. However, the system was not efficient, and often there were shortages of food, medicine, and other important items. This led to the growth of a flourishing black market, in which Russian criminal gangs became heavily involved. Corruption became widespread as the Russian criminals bribed officials into letting them steal goods that they could profitably resell on the black market. Mafiya gangs and Soviet officials collaborated for decades, and a small group of elites became wealthy at the expense of millions of Soviet citizens.

During the 1980s Soviet leader Mikhail Gorbachev tried to reduce corruption and the influence of gangsters by reforming the Communist system. However, the Soviet Union broke apart in 1991 as individual states declared

Convict laborers work on a canal connecting the White Sea and the Baltic Sea, 1930s. Life in the Soviet gulag, a system of prison and work camps, was harsh. Millions of prisoners died in the gulag between 1929 and 1953. Some of the toughest survivors emerged from the gulag as leaders of organized crime in Russia.

their independence. During the 1990s the mafiya groups gained even more power, as life in the former Soviet states became chaotic. Former soldiers and members of the KGB (secret police) gravitated to the mobs. In their book *Organized Crime*, authors Michael Lyman and Gary Potter observed:

> Reminiscent of the Prohibition era in the United States, hundreds, possibly thousands, of large and small gangs deal in drugs and raw materials, extort money, and steal, as the underpaid and often corrupt police look on. High-ranking Russian government officials are also enriching themselves by aligning with known criminals.

The mafiya wasn't content to operate only in Russia, either. Criminal gangs set up operations in many countries, partic-ularly the other 14 former Soviet republics, which were now independent. In states like Armenia, Azerbaijan, Belarus, Georgia, Lithuania, and Ukraine, organized crime figures quickly gained influence over the newly established governments. The mafiya also spread into former Soviet satellites like Poland, Hungary, the Czech Republic, and Slovakia, as well as into western Europe. Today the Russian mafiya is active in at least 50 countries.

Russian mobsters had begun expanding their operations into the United States even before the collapse of the Soviet Union. Immigrants with ties to Russian organized crime families had begun coming to the United States in the 1970s. Many settled in the Brighton

Russian gangster Vyacheslav Ivankov came to the United States in 1992 to take over the mafiya's organized crime operations. His gang was based in Brighton Beach, where Ivankov became known as the "Russian godfather." In 1996, he was convicted of extortion and sentenced to nine years in a federal prison. After his release in 2004 Ivankov was deported to Russia, where he continued his criminal activities. In 2009 he was assassinated, allegedly by a rival mob boss as part of a gang war.

Beach area of Brooklyn, which soon became known as "Little Russia," or sometimes "Little Odessa" after a popular resort city on the Black Sea.

The number of Russian criminals immigrating to the United States increased dramatically after the Soviet Union broke apart. "The ones coming in now are more violent and better organized than the old-timers," noted FBI agent Jim E. Moody in a 1994 report. "They are maintaining links to gangs in Moscow and other places in the old Soviet Union with money flowing back and forth."

The new arrivals didn't waste time making their mark. They quickly figured out ways to defraud American citizens, as well as the government, sometimes in cooperation with the Italian-American crime families. One gas-tax scam has brought in billions of dollars for the Russian mob. Mafiya members would sell fuel at cheap prices to gas stations, telling them that they would take care

In 1995 a group of 25 Russian mobsters was indicted for evading approximately $140 million in federal and state taxes on more than $500 million in fuel sales. The success of that scheme has made the gas-tax scam a popular one for mafiya groups.

of paying the federal fuel taxes, which can add up to 40 percent to the cost of a gallon of gas. The Russian mobsters set up dummy corporations to control the money. They filed all the official paperwork, including false tax returns, but never paid the taxes. These companies would disappear long before federal authorities began looking for them, taking the money with them.

The gas-tax scam is one of many illegal money-making schemes connected with the Russian mob. They have become involved in virtually every area associated with organized crime: credit-card scams, extortion, loan-sharking, racketeering, forgery, insurance and medical frauds, the arms trade, and drug trafficking.

The Russian maifya has become so good at laundering money that many non-Russian criminals, such as Latin American drug cartels, use their services in this field. In one famous case, Garri Grigorian, a Russian living in the United States, helped the mafiya laun-

In recent years the mafiya has become more involved in Miami's South Beach, where Russian mobsters have been involved in credit card fraud, extortion, cyber crimes, prostitution, and smuggling drugs and weapons.

der more than $130 million. Grigorian and his associates created two shell companies—corporations that exist only on paper and have no employees and no physical assets. He then opened several bank accounts for those corporations in Utah. The shell companies never conducted any real business. They existed only to create the illusion that transactions to and from their bank accounts were legitimate. Once those accounts were set up, a Moscow bank affiliated with the mafiya used them to transfer funds, hiding the criminal origins of the money. In August 2005, Grigorian was sentenced to 51 months in prison and ordered to pay $17.42 million in restitution to the Russian government.

Another mafiya specialty is murder. Some people maintain that the Russians may be the most brutal of all the organized crime groups operating today. Journalist Robert I. Friedman, who wrote the 2000 book *Red Mafiya: How the Russian Mob Has Invaded America*, notes that "Italian organized crime has an unwritten rule that they don't go after cops. They don't go after prosecutors. They don't go after American journalists. The Russians go after everybody. One retired cop in New York told me, 'They'll shoot you just to see if their gun works.'"

Friedman had firsthand experience about this observation. The Russians

Facade of a Russian bank in St. Petersburg. According to Russian government officials, more than $60 billion a year is taken out of the country by criminals laundering money. Early in 2013, the government of Cyprus began investigating fraud involving that country's banking system and the mafiya.

put a $100,000 contract on him because of his reporting. On several occasions he saw men associated with the Russian mob watching him—as if to say that they could get him any time they wanted. He died of cardiac arrest in 2002,

International criminal organizations have begun to favor 500 Euro notes because they don't take up much room—up to 10 million Euros ($13.3 million US) can easily fit into a small box or suitcase. It is believed that 90 percent of transactions involving 500 Euro bills are connected to criminal activity. The United Nations estimates that $1.6 trillion was laundered globally in 2012, of which about $580 billion was related to drug trafficking and other forms of organized crime.

and his family believes that anxiety over the constant threat to his life may have been a contributing factor.

Two Russian immigrants linked to the mafiya ran a profitable murder ring. In 2001, a group led by Iouri Mikhel and Jurijus Kadamovas kidnapped five wealthy Los Angeles residents, holding them for ransom. Although they were paid more than $1 million in ransom, the kidnappers murdered all five victims, dumping their bodies in a reservoir near Yosemite National Park. When the men were caught, they were in Colorado scouting out more victims. It

later turned out that Mikhel and Kadamovas had previously run a similar operation in Turkey and Cyprus. In 2007 Mikhel and Kadamovas were convicted; they received the death penalty.

A mafiya organization that has become infamous for its involvement in contract killings is Solntsevskaya Bratva. This gang from Tver, a city in Russia, is considered one of the most dangerous criminal organizations in the world. With more than 5,000 members, Solntsevskaya Bratva is generally considered the largest faction of the Russian Mafia. Sergei Mikhailov, the head of this organization, has never been afraid to use force to accomplish his goals.

In 1996, for example, Mikhailov was arrested in Switzerland and charged with involvement in numerous rackets. However, before he could be placed on trial, many key witnesses died or disappeared. As a result, there was not enough evidence to convict the gangster, and he was free to resume his illicit activities. Mikhailov owns many legitimate businesses, which authorities believe he uses to launder the proceeds of his gang's illegal activities.

Another Russian mobster who has been linked to violent attacks is Semion Mogilevich. This Ukranian gangster has used car bombings and assassinations to eliminate rivals and to threaten political leaders to go along with his schemes. His

Today, Ukranian gangster Semion Mogilevich is considered the most powerful Russian mafia boss. He on the FBI's "Most Wanted" list, and the agency has referred to him as "the most dangerous mobster in the world."

organization is based in Budapest, Hungary. Although it does not have as many members as Solntsevskaya Bratva, the Mogilevich group is actually believed to be the most powerful of the Russian mafiya gangs.

Mogilevich, an educated man with a college degree in economics, is both ruthless and highly intelligent. His organization has been involved in arms trafficking, prostitution, extortion, and murder for hire. The FBI believes that Mogilevich is the Russian mafiya's "boss of bosses"—a leader that is powerful enough to influence operations conducted by all the other mafiya gangs. "He has access to so much, including funding, including other criminal organizations, that he can, with a telephone call and order, affect the global economy," explains FBI agent Peter Kowenhoven.

SKATING ON THIN ICE

Some Mafiya-related cases border on the bizarre. In early 2002, Italian police investigating a Russian mobster, Alimzhan Tokhtakhounov, recorded conversations he had involving France's Olympic ice skating team. The mobster allegedly arranged for a French skating judge to give a high score to a Russian figure-skating team. In return, he "guaranteed" that Russian judges would deliver the gold medal in a different event to the French.

At the 2002 Winter Olympics, the Russian pair Yelena Berezhnaya and Anton Sikharulidze won the gold medal by an extremely narrow margin over Canadians Jamie Sale and David Pelletier. A week later, the French team of Marina Anissina and Gwendal Peizerat won the Olympic ice dancing competition—France's first figure skating gold medal since 1932.

French judge Marie-Reine Le Gougne later admitted that she had been pressured to vote for the Russians. She was suspended, and a second gold medal was awarded to Sale and Pelletier. In August 2002 Tokhtakhouno was charged in a New York court with conspiring to fix the Olympics and arrested at his home in Italy. However, the Italian government ultimately refused to extradite Tokhtakhouno to the United States, so he was never placed on trial.

Tokhtakhounov remains involved in organized crime. His trafficking in drugs and stolen vehicles and illegal sale of arms concern investigators much more than his interest in figure skating.

This sign outside a Hong Kong brothel reads: "Young, fresh Hong Kong girls; White, clean Malaysian girls; Beijing women; Luxurious ghost girls from Russia." The Russian mafiya is heavily involved in human trafficking, forcing young women into prostitution in many parts of Asia.

Arms dealing is another area that the Russian mafiya has been heavily involved in since the 1990s. After the collapse of the Soviet Union, Russian mobsters collaborated with former military and government leaders to sell Soviet weapons to foreign countries and criminal groups all over the world. One Russian mobster, Leonid "Tarzan" Fainberg, even tried to arrange the sale of an old Soviet submarine to a Colombian drug lord named Juan Almeida. Fainberg had already sold this cocaine dealer six Soviet helicopters. The submarine could have carried 40 tons of cocaine to the United States on every trip, with relatively little chance of being detected. The Russian gangster was arrested in Miami before the transaction was completed.

Today, Russian gangs are known to transport small arms through Miami, often selling them in unstable African or Latin American countries, or to terrorist

In January 2013, Moscow's most powerful crime boss, Aslan Usoyan, was assassinated as he left a restaurant in Russia's capital. Usoyan's murder left experts concerned that Russian mafiya groups were about to begin a gang war that would have a terrible toll on civilians.

organizations like Hezbollah. At times, drug cartels have traded large amounts of cocaine for weapons and military supplies; the Russians then distribute the drugs and reap a huge profit.

One important difference between the Italian-American mafia and the Russian mafiya is that in Russia and other former Soviet states, the government is inextricably linked with organized crime groups. This gives mafiya groups a degree of protection that the American mafia, even in its heyday, has never enjoyed. Police in Russia, Georgia, and other former Soviet states investigate only the most blatant, obvious crimes, so the leaders of crime families are rarely punished. These police also do not cooperate much with international agencies investigating mafiya activities. This makes it difficult for American and international police agencies to stop the activities of Russian organized crime groups. However, in recent years a growing awareness of the threat that these international gangs pose has led to greater efforts by governments to stop their illicit operations.

One infamous arms dealer with ties to the mafiya is Viktor Bout, a Russian who became known as the "Merchant of Death." Bout (center) is pictured in U.S. custody after being extradited from Thailand in 2010. He was sentenced to 25 years in prison for attempting to sell weapons to a Colombian terrorist group.

CHAPTER NOTES

p. 11:   "any group having some manner . . ." Federal Bureau of Investigation," Organized Crime: Glossary of Terms." http://www.fbi.gov/about-us/investigate/organizedcrime/glossary

p. 16:   "For nearly a thirty-year period . . ." Selwyn Raab, *Five Families: The Rise, Decline, and Resurgence of America's Most Powerful Mafia Empires*. (New York: St. Martin's Press, 2005), p. 35.

p. 18:   "the foremost organized . . ." Federal Bureau of Investigation, "Italian Organized Crime Overview." http://www.fbi.gov/about-us/investigate/organizedcrime/italian_mafia

p. 18:   "all of these groups . . ." Federal Bureau of Investigation, "Organized Crime." http://www.fbi.gov/about-us/investigate/organizedcrime/overview

p. 25:   "He was a gabber . . ." Kathleen Don, "How Real Is 'Boardwalk Empire's' Al Capone?" *Salon* (October 11,2010). http://www.salon.com/2010/10/11/boardwalk_empire_al_capone/

p. 26:   "the importance of leading . . ." Marilyn Bardsley, "Al Capone: Chicago's Most Infamous Mob Boss," Crime Library. http://www.trutv.com/library/crime/gangsters_outlaws/mob_bosses/capone/apprentice_3.html

p. 27:   "I make my money . . ." Daniel Boorstin, *The Americans: The Democratic Experience* (New York: Vintage, 1974), p. 84.

p. 27:   "Why, I tried . . ." Ibid., p. 85

p. 29:   "Only Capone kills like that," George "Bugs" Moran, quoted in Laurence Bergreen, *Capone: The Man and the Era* (New York: Simon and Schuster, 1994), p. 315.

p. 31:   "Do you know..." Carl Sifakis, *The Mafia Encyclopedia*, 3rd. ed. (New York: Facts on File, 2005), p. 476.

p. 32:   "Al? He's nuttier . . ." Jake Guzik, quoted in Robert Sullivan, ed., *Mobsters and Gangsters: Organized Crime in America from Al Capone to Tony Soprano*. (New York: Life Books, 2002), p. 39.

p. 33:   "Rothstein is recognized . . ." Robert A. Rockaway, *But He Was Good to His Mother: The Life and Crimes of Jewish Gangsters* (Jerusalem: Gefen Publishing, 2000), p. 9.

p. 34:   "I'd do all the homework . . ." David Pietrusza, *Rothstein: The Life, Times, and Murder of the Criminal Genius Who Fixed the 1919 World Series* (New York: Basic Books, 2011), p.19.

p. 35:   "Known along Broadway . . ." Raab, *Five Families*, p. 40.

p. 35:   "Money talks . . ." Lunde, *Organized Crime*, p. 149.

p. 36:   "[Rothstein] taught me how . . ." Rockaway, *But He Was Good to His Mother*, p. 13.

p. 40:   "The FBI describes . . ." Edna Buchanan, "Lucky Luciano: Criminal Mastermind," *Time* (December 7, 1998). http://www.time.com/time/magazine/article/0,9171,989779-1,00.html

p. 40:   "After winning..." Joe Sharkey, "Lucky Luciano: How to Get Ahead by Busting Heads, Breaking Fingers and Dressing Neatly," *New York Times* (December 13, 1998). http://www.nytimes.com/1998/12/13/weekinreview/word-for-word-lucky-luciano-get-ahead-busting-heads-breaking-fingers-dressing.html

p. 49:   "He would have . . ." quoted in "Meyer Lansky Is Dead at 81; Financial Wizard of Organized Crime," *New York Times* (January 16, 1983). http://www.nytimes.com/1983/01/16/obituaries/meyer-lansky-is-dead-at-81-financial-wizard-of-organized-crime.html

p. 50:   "We sat talking . . ." Pietrusza, *Rothstein*, p. 197.

p. 51:   "They were the perfect..." Sifakis, *The Mafia Encyclopedia*, p. 250.

p. 53:   "Lansky was smart . . ." Gary Cohen, "The Lost Journals of Meyer Lansky," American Mafia.com (January 2006). http://www.americanmafia.com/Feature_Articles_331.html

p. 54:   "They're tainted, those boys . . ." Rockaway, *But He Was Good to His Mother*, p. 77.

p. 54:   "The boys snatched . . ." Mark Gribben, "The Purple Gang," Crime Library. http://www.trutv.com/library/crime/gangsters_outlaws/gang/purple/2.html

p. 55:   "They were a predatory . . ." John William Tuohy, "The Purple Gang: An Interview with Paul Kavieff," American Mafia.com. http://www.americanmafia.com/Feature_Articles_50.html

p. 61:   "A self-creation, Mickey . . ." L.M. Harnisch, "Mickey Cohen on the Record—Talking With Author Tere Tereba," *Los Angeles Daily Mirror* (July 26, 2012). http://ladailymirror.com/2012/07/26/mickey-cohen-on-the-record-talking-with-author-tere-tereba/

p. 63:   "Nobody could pay . . ." Rockaway, *But He Was Good to His Mother*, p. 236.

p. 63:   "I took over . . ." Mark Gribben, "Mickey Cohen," Crime Library. http://www.trutv.com/library/crime/gangsters_outlaws/mob_bosses/mickey_cohen/5.html

p. 64:   "I take my oath . . ." quoted in "Trouble in Los Angeles," *Life* (January 16, 1950), p. 80.

p. 64:   "Is it not a fact . . ." Mark Gribben, "Mickey Cohen," Crime Library. http://www.trutv.com/library/crime/gangsters_outlaws/mob_bosses/mickey_cohen/6.html

p. 64:   "Mickey maintained . . ." John Buntin, *L.A. Noir: The Struggle for the Soul of America's Most Seductive City* (New York: Crown Publishing, 2009), p. 160.

p. 65:   "I have killed..." Sifakis, The Mafia Encyclopedia, Third Edition, p. 104.

p. 67   "took an intricately structured . . ." Peter Maas, *Underboss: Sammy the Bull Gravano's Story of Life in the Mafia* (New York: HarperCollins, 1997), p. 213.

p. 67   "Gotti thoroughly dominated . . ." Steve Fishman, "We're Going to Take Over F---ing Hollywood," *New York* (September 16, 2012). http://nymag.com/news/features/john-gotti-jr-2012-9/

p. 68:   "squirrel of a man . . ." Sifakis, *The Mafia Encyclopedia*, p. 180.

p. 70:   "Sure, I'm the boss..." Maas, *Underboss*, p. 213.

p. 70:   "*The Godfather* gave . . ." Nicholas Pileggi, quoted in Jack Newfield, "Little Big Man," *New York*, (June 24, 2002). http://nymag.com/nymetro/news/trends/columns/cityside/6160/

p. 71:   "You know why . . ." Anthony Bruno, "The Gambino Family," Crime Library. http://www.trutv.com/library/crime/gangsters_outlaws/family_epics/gambino/5.html

p. 72:   "The Teflon is gone . . ." Ron Nordland, "The 'Velcro Don': Wiseguys Finish Last," *Newsweek* (April 12, 1992). http://www.thedailybeast.com/newsweek/1992/04/12/the-velcro-don-wiseguys-finish-last.html

p. 72:   "I am writing..." Sifakis, *The Mafia Encyclopedia*, p. 203.

p. 76:   "Reminiscent of the Prohibition era . . ." Lyman and Potter, *Organized Crime*, p. 307

p. 77:   ""The ones coming in now . . ." Selwyn Raab, "Influx of Russian Gangsters Troubles F.B.I. in Brooklyn," *New York Times* (August 23, 1994). http://www.nytimes.com/1994/08/23/nyregion/influx-of-russian-gangsters-troubles-fbi-in-brooklyn.html?src=pm

p. 79:   ""Italian organized crime has an unwritten rule . . ." Robert I. Friedman, quoted in "Russian Mafia's Worldwide Grip," CBS News, February 11, 2009. http://www.cbsnews.com/2100-202_162-217683.html

p. 81:   "most dangerous mobster . . ." Jeanne Meserve, "FBI: Mobster more powerful than Gotti," CNN.com (October 24, 2009). http://www.cnn.com/2009/CRIME/10/21/mogilevich.fbi.most.wanted/index.html

p. 81:   "He has access to so much . . ." Ibid.

GLOSSARY

black market—an underground market for illegal goods, which operates outside of government regulations.

bookmaker—a person who accepts illegal gambling bets. Bookmakers are also known as "bookies."

bootlegging—term for someone who made or sold liquor illegally during the Prohibition era.

bribery—the act of giving a person who holds a public office, such as a judge or policeman, money or something of value so that the person will act in the way that benefits the briber.

caporegime—a high-ranking member of a crime family, who leads a group of "soldiers" and has significant influence and social status within the family. Often abbreviated as "capo."

contract killing—a form of murder in which a person (or group) that wants a target individual killed pays a third party to carry out the killing. Contract killings are common in organized crime because by involving a third party, it is difficult for investigators to prove that the mobster who actually ordered the killing was involved.

extortion—a crime in which one person forces another to give him money. The extortionist may threaten to physically harm the victim or his family, or to damage his property or livelihood, if the victim does not comply.

house—slang term for a casino or other facility that runs games of chance for gamblers.

indict—to formally charge a person or group of people with a crime. Often, an indictment is required before the person can be arrested and placed on trial for the crime.

informant—someone with knowledge of a crime who cooperates with police by providing information about the crime and who committed it.

La Cosa Nostra—Sicilian for "our thing"; another name for the Italian-American Mafia.

Mafia—a popular name for the network of Italian-American crime organizations, also called *la cosa nostra*. The term "Mafia" has also been applied to organized crime networks run by other ethnic groups.

money laundering—processing stolen or dishonest money in order to conceal where it originally came from.

pogrom—an organized massacre of members of a particular ethnic group. In Russia, Jews were the victim of pogroms during the late 19th and early 20th centuries.

Prohibition—name for the period from 1920 to 1933 when the manufacture and distribution of alcohol was illegal in the United States.

prostitution—the crime of performing sex acts for money.

protégé—a person who is trained or educated by a more experienced person, usually called a mentor.

racketeering—a term used to describe the illegal activities of crime families. A *racket* is an illegal business or scheme, such as prostitution, gambling, protection, and drug trafficking.

speakeasy—a nightclub that sells alcohol illegally, especially during the Prohibition period.

surveillance—intense and often secret observation of people who are suspected of criminal behavior, so that law enforcement agencies can develop proof of their illegal activities.

wiretap—a device that cuts in on a telephone wire to enable people to listen to conversations held on the line.

FURTHER READING

Glenny, Misha. *McMafia: A Journey through the Global Criminal Underworld.* New York: Alfred A. Knopf, 2008.

Kavieff, Paul. *The Violent Years: Prohibition and the Detroit Mobs.* Fort Lee, N.J.: Barricade Books, 2001.

Lunde, Paul. *Organized Crime: An Inside Guide to the World's Most Successful Industry.* New York: Barnes and Noble, 2004.

Lyman, Michael D., and Gary W. Potter. *Organized Crime*, 4th ed. Upper Saddle River, N.J.: Pearson Education, 2010.

Montague, Art. *Meyer Lansky: The Shadowy Exploits of New York's Master Manipulator.* Alberta, Canada: Altitude Publishing, 2005.

Raab, Selwyn. *Five Families: The Rise, Decline, and Resurgence of America's Most Powerful Mafia Empires.* New York: St. Martin's Press, 2005.

Reppetto, Thomas. *American Mafia: A History of Its Rise to Power.* New York: Henry Holt and Company, 2004.

Reppetto, Thomas. *Bringing Down the Mob: The War Against the American Mafia.* New York: Henry Holt and Company, 2006.

Rockaway, Robert A. *But He Was Good to His Mother: The Lives and Crimes of Jewish Gangsters.* Jerusalem: Gefen Publishing House, 2000.

Sifakis, Carl. *The Mafia Encyclopedia*, 3rd ed. New York: Facts on File, 2005.

Tereba, Tere. *Mickey Cohen: The Life and Crimes of L.A.'s Notorious Mobster.* Toronto: ECW Press, 2012.

INTERNET RESOURCES

http://www.fbi.gov/hq/cid/orgcrime/ocshome.htm

The organized crime section of the FBI's official website has many links to detailed information on important cases and particular kinds of crimes in this area.

http://www.trutv.com/library/crime/gangsters_outlaws/index.html

The Crime Library website includes articles about the history of the Mafia, Prohibition, and biographies of many infamous gangsters, including Al Capone, John Gotti, the Purple Gang, and Arnold Rothstein.

http://www.history.com/topics/mafia-in-the-united-states

The History Channel provides information about the history of the Mafia in the United States.

http://www.unodc.org/unodc/en/organized-crime/index.html

The United Nations Office on Drugs and Crime provides this website with information about the global reach of organized crime groups.

http://www.nij.gov/topics/crime/transnational-organized-crime/major-groups.htm

A branch of the U.S. Department of Justice created this survey of major organized crime groups that have an international scope.

http://chicagohs.org/history/capone.html

The Chicago Historical Society hosts this website which contains biographical information about Al Capone and the Chicago Outfit, as well as photographs and links to primary sources.

http://chicagohs.org/history/blacksox.html

The fixing of the 1919 World Series, which Arnold Rothstein is believed to have been involved in, is discussed in detail on this website hosted by the Chicago Historical Society.

http://www.fbi.gov/about-us/history/famous-cases/al-capone/al-capone

The FBI's biography of Al Capone details how the U.S. Treasury Department brought down the infamous mobster.

http://www.biography.com/people/bugsy-siegel-9542063

A&E Biography profile of Benjamin "Bugsy" Siegel, who ran Murder Inc. and helped bring the mob to Las Vegas.

http://www.time.com/time/magazine/article/0,9171,989779,00.html

Biographical article on Charles "Lucky" Luciano from *Time* magazine's 1998 list of "100 Remarkable People of the 20th Century."

http://www.unodc.org/unodc/money-laundering/index.html

The United Nations Office on Drugs and Crime provides this website with information about money laundering and steps that governments and financial institutions can take to stop it.

INDEX

Numbers in **bold italics** refer to captions.

About the Author: Jim Whiting has written more than 100 non-fiction books for young adults and edited over 150 others. He lives near Seattle, Washington.